Rebel Music

Resistance through Hip Hop and Punk

A volume in
Critical Constructions: Studies on Education and Society
Curry Malott, *Series Editor*

Rebel Music

Resistance through Hip Hop and Punk

edited by

Priya Parmar
Brooklyn College–CUNY

Anthony J. Nocella, II
Hamline University

Scott Robertson
University of California, Los Angeles

Martha Diaz
New York University

INFORMATION AGE PUBLISHING, INC.
Charlotte, NC • www.infoagepub.com

Library of Congress Cataloging-in-Publication Data

A CIP record for this book is available from the Library of Congress
http://www.loc.gov

ISBN: 978-1-62396-909-7 (Paperback)
978-1-62396-910-3 (Hardcover)
978-1-62396-911-0 (ebook)

Printed in the United States of America

This book is dedicated to all those youth who have been marginalized, locked up, kicked out, murdered, or have taken their own lives while resisting and rebelling against all that is oppressive.

CONTENTS

PART III

RESISTANCE

PART IV

REBELLION

PART V

REPRESSION

PART VI

EXPRESSION

PART VII

RESPECT

PART VIII

COMMUNITY

FOREWORD

Chuck D

Being born in Queens, New York in 1960 gave me some great cultural advantages. It was a period of social and cultural change, the truest definition of revolution as far as I'm concerned. The area was ripe for music and art saying *it* like it had to be said. I come from parents who collected records, were signed up to record clubs, and were ever present consumers during the peak of the soul era. Not only were big black 33 RPM discs from record labels such as Motown, Stax, Atlantic, Columbia, and Chess on the floor, but also jazz discs, not to mention comedy records like Redd Foxx and Moms Mabley. Strewn among all these were the small records with the big hole in the middle, the 45RPM disc.

Being born with "negro" on my New York state birth certificate, over the course of a decade, I witnessed my family go from being classified as "negro" to "colored" by the time I reached the first grade in 1966. A year after the Civil Rights bill was agreed upon, it was changed to "Black" with a capital B for *beautiful* by 1968. It seemed apparent that this new category was spawned from just one amazing man and his blazing music and band: the godfather of soul, Mr. James Brown. I have written many times about that man and that record's impact. Motown, even before Marvin Gaye's "What's Going On," had "War" by Edwin Starr, "Love Child" by The Supremes; hell, even "Wake Me" meant something to some of my people by 1969. It was understood by the time I was five that music had to be a bit more than merely recreational to reflect the social time. It was an accumulation of rage, reflection, rhythm, and riot. What Bob Dylan dared off the heels of the beat

Rebel Music, pages xi–xii

poets was punk. How could it not be? It was the peoples' music—an unsatisfied people—smacking and challenging the elite, perhaps with more than words and music but sharing the vibe of activity.

By the time I was ten in 1970, music seized the expressway into the heads as much as the songs striking the hearts. The decade of overt assassinations, war, discrimination, and sexism was supposedly over as USA claimed the damn moon. But the genie was out of the bottle in many cases. The vocals were now quicker to answer Huntley and Brinkley and Walter Cronkite's mega-networked words. By that decade, my intrigue into Black history and all history led me into discovering for myself punk before punk. There was music that chose to punk out and pick out, and thus identify, the status quo. Billie Holiday's "Strange Fruit." Josh White's music, they are not. Gospel songs that dared to pin the damn devil. The roots of Pop Staples letting his daughters know they could sing songs against what they saw wrong. From the words of Ginsberg, to feeling the song titles' notes of jazz blues guitarist Grant Green, to the straight out intention of Archie Shepp's free jazz stylings. Then it got confrontational with configuration and creative changes. In my opinion, rap music and Hip Hop were tailor-made to answer to the concrete poured in the 1980s for this millennial new *whirl odor.*

Entering college freshman year of 1978 there was a lot of lying going on, I thought. As a school cartoonist, I was interested in art and cultural audacity. Socially I was fresh and green, and although I wasn't yet involved with music, I was tipping over with it. Hip Hop as a recording music bit me. Hard. Social conscious songs like Brother D's "How We Gonna Make the Black Nation Rise" only reminded me of what I had in myself. By 22, I was ripe and ready for Grandmaster Flash and The Furious Five's "The Message" in 1982. It was a culmination of understanding what the damn music was for, alongside its recreational intention. All this is to say that social activity by real people doing real things is what steered these artists to say what the streets couldn't say succinctly. That's also punk. But the movement of the music cannot zoom by the needs of the people and reflect the lack of principle that the elite class has exhibited.

Eventually politics will crumble in the wake of not being true enough to any essential mass cause. Thus, why are we surprised today when the lack of any movement, much less a rebellious punk movement, has so many witnessing the effect of mainstream music melting into meaningless mush before our very ears? This book will really be in tune with what has already been shown and proven. It will prove that the future of rebel, Hip Hop, and punk cultures choose the directions as powerful as their past.

Always *PE*ace and res*PE*ct,
Chuck D
Co-founder of Public Enemy

FOREWORD

Chris Hannah

> *The elites and their courtiers in the liberal class always condemn the rebel as impractical. They dismiss the stance of the rebel as counterproductive. They chastise the rebel for being angry. The elites and their apologists call for calm, reason, and patience. They use the hypocritical language of compromise, generosity, and understanding to argue that we must accept and work with the systems of power. The rebel, however, is beholden to a moral commitment that makes it impossible to compromise. The rebel refuses to be bought off with foundation grants, invitations to the White House, television appearances, book contracts, academic appointments, or empty rhetoric. The rebel is not concerned with self-promotion or public opinion. The rebel knows that, as Augustine wrote, hope has two beautiful daughters, anger and courage—anger at the way things are and the courage to change them. The rebel knows that virtue is not rewarded. The act of rebellion justifies itself.*
>
> —Chris Hedges, *Death of the Liberal Class* (2010, p. 215)

There's a famous scene in the film *The Matrix* where Morpheus (Laurence Fishburne) offers Neo (Keanu Reeves) a choice between ingesting a blue pill and a red pill. If he chooses the blue pill his memory of the event will be erased and he will wake up in his bed as if nothing has happened and continue to believe in the illusion generated by the Matrix. But if he takes the red pill he will irrevocably see the world as it *really* is, however painful and terrifying that may be. Many of us, if we look back over our lives, have had a red pill/blue pill moment of our own—a moment where we finally see the prevailing order for what it really is: a real-time dystopian insanity

Rebel Music, pages xiii–xvi

rather than the force for liberty and justice we have been conditioned to believe it to be.

My own date with Morpheus came on a warm, early 1980s summer afternoon on the Canadian prairies while sitting in front of my friend's record player in his parents' living room. I was just 15 years old, the son of a Cold War fighter pilot, and had spent most of my life living on military installations, immersed in and obsessed with the culture and technology of war. I had seen little of the world and knew next to nothing about it but was convinced that justice and liberty were things that could only be secured by overwhelming military might and obedience to the state. I believed that anyone outside this worldview was a traitor.

As my friend set an LP down on the turntable and handed me the accompanying record cover, the speakers exploded with a barrage of sound that was as frantic and jarring as anything I had ever heard in my life. I sat in stunned silence as an obscure punk band called Millions of Dead Cops rampaged through an ear-splitting nine minutes of sonic pandemonium, brazenly assaulting every facet of the prevailing order I was brought up to venerate: police, corporations, state power, patriotism, manhood, obedience to social norms—all completely and utterly eviscerated in the course of one shockingly brief side of an LP. It was outrageous, offensive, and treasonous, and I told my friend so. I shook my head and told him it wasn't for me.

But as I left his house, something nagged at me all the way home. I was bothered by what I'd just heard. How could a band sound so unhinged? How could they be so enraged? What the hell were they talking about anyways? Comparing the police to the Ku Klux Klan? Talking about wearing women's clothes and railing against "queer-bashers"? Calling John Wayne a Nazi? What the fuck was this pinko commie bullshit? Why would they say stuff like that? It was insane. It was nonsense. And it sure as hell wasn't for me. I was safe and secure in my worldview and had no interest in making anything more complicated for myself.

But, of course, it was already too late. The offer had been made. Morpheus had shown me the door, and it was going to be impossible to resist stepping through it, even just for a moment, just to see. The next thing I knew I was at the record store turning the LP over and over in my hands, shaking my head at the song-titles on the back, all the while slowly making my way to the cash register. Nothing was ever the same again.

More than ever, it is easy to be fooled by the illusion. The maxim of "garbage in, garbage out" prevails. The celebrity culture, the "reality" programming, the political spectacle, the celebration of humiliation, the ascendancy of rape culture, the fetishization of war—these all combine to create a society of innumerate, illiterate, disconnected hyper-consumers. It kills the citizen. We become human garbage.

Often, as young people, we find ourselves on our own in all this with seemingly no hope of escape. But once in a while, as the never-ending tsunami of garbage roils over us, we catch a glimpse of something out of the corner of our eyes, something barely visible that stands out against the sewage. At first we're unsure of it. It's different. It's unfamiliar. It might be dangerous.

Then we realize that its unfamiliarity is due to the fact that it is valuable. It actually has meaning. We didn't even know what meaning was before this. We grab hold of it, and it pulls us along. It pulls us up. For the first time we see all that garbage for what it really is as we break through the surface. *Rebel Music* is a collection of and meditation on these transcendent musical moments.

I wish them upon everyone.

—Jesus H. Chris/Propagandhi

REFERENCE

Hedges, C. (2010). *Death of the liberal class.* Toronto, Canada: A.A. Knopf Canada.

ACKNOWLEDGEMENTS

Rebel Music would not be possible without the many brilliant and great Hip Hop and punk creators who have paved a path towards the global communities we have today. We would also like to thank everyone at Information Age Publishing and the series editor Curry Malott, a wonderful scholar and human being. We would like to give love to our family and friends who have supported us, challenged us, and laughed with us over the many years on this planet. We would also like to thank the brilliant and powerful contributors to this book. *Rebel Music...* would not be a reality without Don C. Sawyer III, Hasan Stephens, Zack Furness, Noelle Chaddock, Lauren Corman, Sarat Colling, David Stovall, Michael Benitez, Comrade Black, Dru Ryan, Ed Avery-Natale, Daniel White Hodge, Kirby Pringle, Marcella Runell Hall, Ross Haenfler, Emery Petchauer, and Michael Loadenthal. We would like to give great appreciation to Chuck D and Chris Hannah for writing the forewords and Kim Socha, Peter McLaren, Ryan Williams-Virden, Mike Park, Steven Blush, David Gabbard, Jason Del Gandio, and Joe Leeson-Schatz for reviewing this book on such a short deadline. Finally, we would like to thank each other, the editors, for the collaboration, creativity, the long talks, many e-mails, and struggle to make this important book come to life! We hope that *Rebel Music* will create consciousness and inspire youth, teachers, professors, community organizers, artists, and lovers of Hip Hop and punk to take action against social injustices.

Rebel Music, page xvii

INTRODUCTION

Priya Parmar, Anthony J. Nocella II, Scott Robertson, and Martha Diaz

I rebel music.
Why can't we roam this open country?
Oh, why can't we be what we wanna be?
We want to be free.
—Bob Marley, "Rebel Music"

Today youth are living in a world in which they must be able to think, act, and perform quickly, while simultaneously perusing social media sites, listening to their iPods, typing on their laptops or iPads, tweeting on Twitter, posting on Instagram, or texting on their cell-phones. As influential philosopher, educator, and activist Paulo Freire advocated, to successfully engage with youth, one must know what they are concerned with and interested and invested in, rather than believing the teacher is the savior or sole expert in student knowledge (Freire, 1973, 1998). *Rebel Music,* rooted in marginalized rebel youth community, is for educators, activists, and scholars who work with both youth in general and those youth whose lives are situated within the punk and Hip Hop communities to learn with and from other Hip Hop and punk youth, activists, artists, educators, and scholars in their communities about identity, culture, and politics. Too often we listen to the beats, but not to the lyrics of the artist, glazing over the powerful message construction that underscores the song. This very important, unique, and captivating book takes the reader through a series of fun, educational chapters that offer theoretically-informed textual analyses of Hip Hop and

Rebel Music, pages xix–xxviii

punk lyrics and artists. The eight sections do not address the two genres separately, but rather bring the two very similar youth cultures together. Hip Hop and punk, that is, having emerged in the same reactionary era in a wide range of communities of working people, seem to have been driven by much of the same anger, rage, and rebellion. Consequently, it might be accurate to argue that Hip Hop and punk are more similar than different. This analysis is important for developing a pedagogy of unity for the 21st century.

THE ENVIRONMENT OF CULTURAL IRRELEVANT EDUCATION

The current educational landscape is set up in which mundane, standard, test-driven, rule-bound, and mechanistic routines are the norm. In other words, as a result of neoliberal politics, technocratic and positivist reform efforts such as No Child Left Behind, Race to the Top, and more recently, the Common Core Standards, teaching has been reduced to learning or acquiring a set of skills. This reductionary approach to education pushes teachers to use their time wisely and efficiently in a way that forces rote learning, memorization, and drilling of skills necessary to pass standardized exams. Oftentimes the result is decontextualized content that is rendered meaningless and boring. If students are not acting out due to boredom, they are passively sitting by, trained to behave according to a set of rules and standards that ultimately produce compliant, complacent citizens who know their "place" (Au, 2009). Is this the type of educational environment we want to support? Or, do we wish to provide democratic education where the goal is to create civic-minded, critical thinkers that are socially, culturally, economically, and politically active in society?

Based on the foundation of critical pedagogy, *Rebel Music: Resistance through Hip Hop and Punk* challenges positivist educational traditions, arguing for a fair, just, and inclusive curricula that represents multiple and alternative perspectives and knowledge. *Rebel Music* represents a collection of multiple and alternative lyrics from select Hip Hop and punk artists who we found many of the youth we work with listen to and are influenced by. But why take seriously *what*, and *whom*, our students are influenced by? Ignoring, excluding, or marginalizing these "other" perspectives and knowledge centralizes or confirms certain cultures while devaluing others. The valuing of particular forms of knowledge, language, and experience familiar only to certain (privileged) ideologies are legitimized, thereby reproducing what French sociologist, Pierre Bourdieu refers to as "cultural capital" or cultural reproduction (Aronowitz & Giroux, 1993).

HIP HOP HISTORY

Hip Hop culture was born out of cultural, socio-economic, and political resistance about 40 years ago (Fricke & Ahearn, 2002; Chang, 2005). Poor and blue-collar working class Black, Latino, and white youth—many first-and-second-generation immigrants of Caribbean and Latin American backgrounds—refused to succumb to the inequality, violence, and degradation of the Bronx, NY. Like so many flagship cities across the United States in the 1970s, New York City was plagued with poverty, unemployment, organized gangs and crime, prostitution, and an epidemic of arson and drugs. The narrative in the press was bleak and dangerous. The media character assassination and criminalization of Black and Brown youth could be seen depicted in popular culture such as in the movies "The Warriors" and "Fort Apache, The Bronx."

As a way to contest and challenge the corrupt system, teenagers came together to create an alternative existence, identity, and voice. What seemed to outsiders as a subversive subculture, Hip Hop offered its participants a safe haven, community of peers, tools, new skills, and opportunities to learn. Young people were able to create art, launch businesses, and speak up for a generation about oppression, poverty, and injustice. Hip *Hoppas*, with their own vernacular, freestyle moves, and street flavor reinvented and changed politics, entertainment, technology, entrepreneurship, fashion, fine art, education, and spirituality. The Hip Hop generation gained the freedom and courage to do so from the Civil Rights generation, Black Power and Liberation Movement, and Black Arts Movement.

The four most popular artistic elements of Hip Hop provide different ways of expression and points of entry into the culture. With little to no resources, you could participate and get in the Hip Hop cypher by DJing, B-Boying/Girling (a.k.a. break dancing), MCing, rapping or spoken word, and writing (i.e., graffiti). Once you enter the cipher you must be able to *show and prove* to keep your place. Your artistic craft, skills, style, and intentions are always being challenged. Coined by the godfather of Hip Hop, Afrika Bambaataa, the "fifth element," knowledge of self and the community, gave the other elements purpose and meaning to the art and culture. It is through this critical analysis, counter-narrative, and do-it-yourself *by any means necessary* mindset that Hip Hop grew and spread throughout the planet.

Through the lens of the MC/rapper, audiences can hear the stories of the victim, perpetrator, and eyewitness. Public Enemy front man Chuck D once referred to rap music as the CNN of the streets. With ferocious storytelling wit, grit, and bravado, the MC indulged you with history, anecdotes, and dreams of a better future. Inspired by their predecessors, The Last Poets, Gil Scott Heron, and James Brown, the pioneers of Hip Hop music sparked a critical conscious "rebelution" that continues to this day.

Unfortunately, cooptation by big business has taken its toll, and many artists we hear today on the radio are no longer cut from the same cloth. But as the music industry model is forced to evolve or die by the advancements of technology and conscious artists, a robust underground independent scene is once again growing and triggering a new form of resistance.

PUNK HISTORY

Punk came out of the politics and rock and roll of the 1960s. Punk rockers tended to come from the more privileged, white working-class communities, who, like their African American and Latino counterparts, also began to feel the economic and cultural squeeze of the neoliberal era starting in the 1970s. Punk rock was therefore not surprisingly rooted in rebellion, resistance, and revolt, and therefore stigmatized by adult society as deviant, delinquent, and demonic. Starting in the 1970s in the United States, Europe, and Australia, and emerging simultaneously *with* and *alongside* Hip Hop, punk was loud, in your face, and defiant. The foundational theme was questioning authority. Like Hip Hop, punk had many subcultures within it such as political punk, pop punk, crust punk, metal punk, hardcore, Oi! punk, and riot grrrl punk (which was feminist grounded). This list continues to grow today. Punk in the beginning had three commonalities among punks—fashion, attitude, and music. The music of course had to be punk, which meant loud, fast, and angry. Fashion was typically dirty, worn out clothes, often black with bright colored hair or a shaved head and piercings and tattoos. Each sub group had differing styles. For example, skinheads could be spotted wearing suspenders and Doc Martens. The fashion ran counter to the mainstream. The higher the shock value, the better the look. Finally, the attitude had to be an "I don't care what you say. I will do it anyway and do it the way I want." This attitude is grounded in the philosophy of "do-it-yourself," commonly known as DIY.

Punk's DIY politics and attitude came out of the emergence of a new wave of anarchists in the post-1960s era. This punk movement included drugs and alcohol, random sexual encounters, destruction of property, patches and metal spikes on one's clothing, and the distribution of zines at music shows or protests. Anarchism was first shaped into a theory by William Godwin. While there are many types of anarchism, even anarchist-capitalist, the philosophy and movement challenges all domination and authoritarianism. Anarchism promotes a mutual-aid sharing anti-ownership economy, while promoting a direct democracy and collective-based political structure (Amster, DeLeon, Fernandez, Nocella, & Shannon, 2009).

The punk ideology that spread in white suburbia shifted to communities of color in the U.S. and has now spread globally. Chicano bands from East

Los Angeles sing of oppression that punk rockers in Indonesia can relate with. Although there are and have been punk rock movements that are overtly racist and sexist, punk rock also acts as a critique from within. Punk rock in England was once a battleground of neo-Nazi bands and anarchist bands dueling lyrically and with fists. The best critiques of punk rock come from punk rock. This is what has historically made punk rock meaningful for youth grappling with issues from their own community to the world at large. Punk can lament the loss of community to the loss of innocence in war. It can challenge masculinity, sexism, racism, homophobia, classism, and speciesism. Punk can be the proverbial wrench in the gears of mainstream ideology. Punk is no longer, if it ever really was, a white suburban pastime.

THE VALUE OF HIP HOP AND PUNK

While *Rebel Music* acknowledges Hip Hop and punk as cultures, this anthology will focus solely on the music element of each by critically analyzing lyrics that critique, resist, and rebel against oppressive forces that are intricately—and intentionally—constructed by dominant paradigms. The artists selected for critique *speak* to youth; therefore this book will ultimately *speak* to youth as well. The artists chosen for critique have in one way or another transcended mainstream and stereotypical (mis)perceptions of their respective cultures to represent a voice for marginalized groups in the form of social and political protest, speaking out against oppressive hegemonic conditions (from everyday life in the neighborhood and workplace, to institutions of learning). The examination of Hip Hop and punk lyrics, as a way of challenging dominant ideologies in the construction of culture, identity, and politics, serves as a vehicle of promise, hope, and anger in hopes of inspiring social, economic, and political action for more equitable working, living, and educational conditions (Parmar, 2010). Such a discourse as the critical examination of Hip Hop and punk lyrics—separately and in conjunction with one another—that analyzes and explains the social, cultural, and political factors that foster "deviant" behaviors can help decrease and even eliminate false perceptions and unwarranted fears and stereotypes from those who sit on the outside of Hip Hop and punk cultures, as well as bridge the gap between those within the two cultures who feel they have nothing in common.

As time went on, white youth from the punk community and Black youth from the Hip Hop community started becoming influenced by one another's culture (from the clothes, music, attitude, and politics). For example, both communities began to wear baggie pants, which the youth sagged with similar low-top "fat" shoes during the 1990s. In the 2000s they both started wearing tight jeans with "thin" high-tops and a fashionable belt. Moreover, the shirt designs from logos to fonts in those two decades were very similar.

Additionally, both Hip Hop and punk movements are DIY—do-it-yourself—and both have redefined the "American dream" to suit their needs. In challenging racism, we have chosen not to capitalize "white" throughout the book while intentionally capitalizing "Black," "Brown," and "People of Color" when these identities are mentioned. Further, in this same vein we capitalize Hip Hop and not punk.

ABOUT THIS BOOK

Arguably, some of the artists included in this collection may be deemed unworthy of critical study due to the explicit nature of their lyrics. While the editors of this volume debated and struggled with—for a very long length of time—which artists to include and exclude, we ultimately left it up to the youth we worked with to compile a list of their favorites whom they found to be inspiring, influential, and relatable. To do this, we had to remind ourselves of the role we played as critical pedagogues when working with youth.

Of significant importance to critical educators is changing the teacher-student relationship where the teacher is traditionally viewed as the "expert" to one that is dialogical and interactive. The students are now "experts" teaching the teacher something that may be unfamiliar. Put simply, critical educators must *listen to* and *respect* their students. Even if we find some of the knowledge and experiences students bring into the classroom to be "problematic" or non-educational, we must change our perceptions and engage students in a critical dialogue, viewing both parties as "subjects" to work with and learn from, rather than "objects" to be trained and schooled (Parmar, 2009). Teachers are then more apt to consider the study of popular culture as valid and valuable knowledge because of its direct correlation to students' lives.

Our students left us with a long list of popular artists that (un)fortunately, due to page limitations, required us to narrow down the selection to eight artists representing each culture. The criteria that we used to narrow down the list included our own critical examination of the artist's discography as a whole, not fragmented parts (or select lyrics) that, alone, have catapulted her/him into mainstream media outlets. Sadly, popular artists such as Nicki Minaj and Drake did not make our final Hip Hop list, nor did the Subhumans and Sex Pistols within the punk list.

True to the title of this book, all the artists chosen have recorded lyrics that are "rebellious" to dominant ideologies, where the youth are labeled deviants and delinquents. However, mainstream airwaves—to some extent—have not allowed this rebellious music to reach the masses as today's youth are one of the largest consumers of music. As such, *Rebel Music* will explore the complex—and somewhat contradictory—binary relationship between the artist and their respective industry, examining the power constructs that exist that have some consumers shaking their heads in confusion, resulting in a love-hate feeling for a particular artist. How can an artist, one minute, skyrocket to the top of the charts with an arguably offensive song and the next minute, preach against, say violence or racism, in another song?

Contributors have critically analyzed lyrics keeping in mind that the primary audiences for this book are youth, teachers/professors, and educators who work with youth. Some of the other issues addressed will allow youth and their educators to understand the messages found in the lyrics such as:

- The complex relationship between power and knowledge.
- The ways knowledge is produced, accepted, and rejected.
- The ways individuals receive dominant representations and encodings of the world—are they assimilated, resisted, or transformed?
- The manner in which individuals negotiate their relationship with the "official story," the legitimate canon (Kincheloe & Steinberg, 1997, p. 87).

This sort of critical analysis validates marginalized voices, histories, and experiences and helps youth map their relation to the social worlds around them. They do this by realizing the complex ways in which they are connected to both people like themselves and those radically different from them (Kincheloe & Steinberg, 1997; Parmar, 2009). Deconstructing these lyrics by analyzing, critiquing, and interpreting the complex relationships among power, knowledge, culture, identity, and politics allows youth the opportunity to discuss how power situates itself in their lives, whether it is in school, their neighborhoods, or in the larger society. The production and maintenance of cultural hegemony found within these lyrics are challenged, questioned, and resisted. It is our intention that listening to—*really listening to*—and *respecting* youth culture and identity will provide opportunities for active engagement with diverse groups of people and opportunities for constructing and validating "new" knowledge. We hope this will inspire a sense of autonomy, ownership, and responsibility when making choices and decisions that affect and improve one's own life as well as the lives of others are created. As we have learned from the youth we work with, we hope readers of *Rebel Music* will develop the critical skills necessary to work for a more democratic system, which would ensure equality, justice, freedom, and respect for *all.*

SUMMARY OF THE BOOK

This book begins with two forewords written by two amazing and highly respected individuals in their given music communities: Hip Hop's outspoken cultural critic from the group Public Enemy, Chuck D, and lead vocalist and guitarist from the punk group Propagandhi, Chris Hannah. The book continues with eight interrelated sections designated by a specific theme reflected in the lyrics. Part I of the book is dedicated to oppression. Chapter 1, written by Don C. Sawyer III and Hasan Stephens, encourages readers to employ critical media literacy in this day of global hyper- capitalism, media, and digital technology to analyze and address social, economic, or political issues that will inspire activism. As an example, they critically analyze the song "My Life" by The Game & Lil Wayne to explore the complexities and struggles of Black males living in urban America. Chapter 2, written by Zack Furness on the song "Petroleum Distillation" by Fifteen, is a great example of how the band connects the "political" to the "personal," similar to how Paulo Freire politicized education in liberating Brazilian peasant laborers from economic oppression. Similar to Freire's problem-posing approach to creating consciousness that results in agency (activism), Zach deconstructs "Petroleum Distillation" by uncovering themes of capitalism and pollution as two forms of oppression that once recognized as such, leads to autonomy as freedom from oppression.

Part II of the book is dedicated to marginalization. Chapter 3, written by Noelle Chaddock, argues that Hip Hop is a vehicle to critically examine issues, particularly Black feminism, from a socio-political philosophical lens. Noelle pays homage to women of Hip Hop, focusing particular attention to Queen Latifah's song "Ladies First" in which male dominance, oppression, and female marginalization are challenged within and beyond Hip Hop culture. Chapter 4, written by Lauren Corman and Sarat Colling analyzes the song "Nailing Descartes to the Wall" by Propagandhi. The song forces us to self-reflect on our own contradictory and hypocritical actions; specifically, do we practice what we preach and hold ourselves accountable? The politically—and ethically—charged lyrics challenge us to examine privileged perspectives from multiple and marginalized perspectives. In this case, a close, harsh examination of animal exploitation is revealed ending in a call for an animal liberation movement that leads to a war against the "animals-as-food" industry.

Part III of the book is dedicated to resistance. Chapter 5, written by David Stovall, focuses on the powerful and counter-hegemonic group, Public Enemy. David deconstructs the lyrics of "Fight the Power" by contextualizing the events of the 1980s and analyzing the economic, political, and social conditions affecting Black and Latino/a urban youth. The content of the lyrics—and the symbolism of Public Enemy—transcends time where educators today can develop social justice curricula that address similar issues facing urban youth in hopes of inspiring resistance and agency. Chapter 6, written by Scott Robertson on the song "Hero of War" by Rise Against, is a touching narrative of an American Army soldier chronicling his time fighting in the war against Iraq. As yet another example of a politically-charged punk rock song (and band), Scott critically analyzes the lyrics, revealing how power constructs make war and joining the military an alluring and patriotic duty for youth. Rise Against joins many other punk bands that are anti-war and challenges hegemony by analyzing how war benefits the elite and victimizes those serving in the military—working class youth.

Part IV of the book is dedicated to rebellion. Chapter 7, written by Michael Benitez, focuses on the lyrics "Hip Hop is Dead" by Nas. Michael argues that Hip Hop culture and all of its elements can be educational texts that are transformative in creating critical consciousness and social change. The lyrics of "Hip Hop is Dead" challenge "Hip Hoppas" and artists to take back ownership of the culture that has been commoditized and commercialized by corporate interests. Chapter 8, written by Comrade Black about the song "Pictures of Women Giving Birth Sell Records" by Oi Polloi, echoes the underlying themes permeating from many punk bands: the DIY movement that resulted in a rejection by mainstream, dominant culture to those youth who did not—and would not—comply to mainstream standards and values.

Part V of the book is dedicated to repression. Chapter 9, written by Dru Ryan, focuses on the lyrics of "State Run Radio" by Lupe Fiasco. The lyrics challenge consumers to be conscious and media savvy in recognizing that an illusion of variety and diversity exists in the form of access to songs via mainstream radio stations. "State Run Radio" explicitly exposes the limited choices we have as consumers and artists if listening to only mainstream airwaves and the detrimental effects of it: the dumbing down of knowledge and awareness as consumers that serve to benefit the corporate and elite. Chapter 10, written by Ed Avery-Natale, centers around punk band Goldfinger and their counter-hegemonic lyrics in "Iron Fist," which critique capitalism, industry, and the state.

Part VI of the book is dedicated to expression. Chapter 11, written by Daniel White Hodge, analyzes the song "Fight for Your Right to Party" by the rebellious Hip Hop—but rock, funk, and punk infused—band, the Beastie Boys. Daniel unveils how this group of white "boys" represented the voice and experiences of a marginalized, oppressed, and often forgotten about demographic during the 1970s and particularly 1980s Reagan years: poor and middle class white youth. Chapter 12, written by Kirby Pringle about the song "Terminal Preppie" by Dead Kennedys, is about a rejection of white privilege and elitism; specifically it is using an ironic personal story of a typical white, elite male in college, who wants to drink beer, make money, have a "sexy" wife, and enjoy Christian holidays.

Part VII of the book is dedicated to respect. Chapter 13, by Marcella Runell Hall, analyzes iconic Hip Hop MC Tupac Shakur's timeless hit single "Dear Mama." While the lyrics pay homage to his mother, former Black Panther

Afeni Shakur, Marcella critiques Tupac as an artist who was highly influential in naming oppressive forces and power constructs by revealing social injustices affecting young, urban youth of color. Chapter 14, by Ross Haenfler on the song "Straightedge" by Minor Threat, reflects how punk music moves its audience to *move* towards action. The lyrics represent a call for what is known as a *lifestyle movement*, as we've seen in previous chapters, by making the political personal towards social change. Just as critical scholars in education politicize education, Ross argues that we must politicize our personal choices and provides concrete examples of how we can collectively accomplish this.

Finally, Part VIII of the book is dedicated to community. Chapter 15, written by Emery Petchaur, examines the autobiographical narrative of life in urban South Central Los Angeles from the perspective of Ice Cube in the lyrics "It Was a Good Day." Quite popular in Hip Hop is the autobiographical nature of the music in representing the artist's lived experience. Highlighting various themes often experienced in South Central LA sets the background for the song while political undertones are revealed: death and violence. Chapter 16, written by Michael Loadenthal, centers around the lyrics of "Welcome to Paradise" by Green Day, which explores gentrification and its effects on white youth and their families as they are displaced from their original urban environment into unfamiliar, suburban communities.

REFERENCES

Amster, R., DeLeon, A., Fernandez, L., Nocella II, A. J., & Shannon, D. (2009). *Contemporary anarchist studies: Anthology of anarchy in the academy*. New York, NY: Routledge.

Aronowitz, S., & Giroux, H. (1993). *Education still under siege* (2nd ed). Westport, CT: Bergin & Garvey.

Au, W. (2009). *Unequal by design: High-stakes testing and the standardization of inequality*. New York, NY: Routledge.

Chang, J. (2005). *Can't stop won't stop: A history of the hip hop generation*. New York, NY: St. Martin's Press.

Freire, P. (1973). *Education for critical consciousness*. New York, NY: Continuum.

Freire, P. (1998). *Teachers as cultural workers: Letters to those who dare teach*. Boulder, CO: Westview Press.

Fricke, J. & Ahearn, C. (2002). *Yes yes y'all: Oral history of hip-hop's first decade*. New York, NY: Persues Press.

Kincheloe, J., & Steinberg S. (1997). *Changing multiculturalism*. Buckingham, UK: Open University Press.

Parmar, P. (2010). "Does hip hop have a home in urban education?" In S. Steinberg (Ed.). *19 Urban questions: Teaching in the city* (2nd ed.). New York, NY: Peter Lang.

Parmar, P. (2009). *Knowledge reigns supreme: The critical pedagogy of hip hop activist KRS-ONE*. Rotterdam, NL: Sense Publishers.

PART I

OPPRESSION

CHAPTER 1

"MY LIFE" BY THE GAME & LIL WAYNE

Don C. Sawyer III
Hasan Stephens

I have been crucified with Christ; it is no longer I who live, but Christ lives in me; and the life which I now live in the flesh I live by faith in the Son of God, who loved me and gave Himself for me.

—Galatians 2:20

At the end of the "My Life" music video there is a scene with Game and some of his homies in a cemetery after seeing many of their friends taken away from them through senseless acts of violence. This seemed like a space they frequented often to lay an ever increasing number of friends to rest. During the last scene, the camera pans across a few members of the crew and catches a glimpse of the sky with the above scripture in the clouds. Some may ask, How could a rapper like Game end his video with scripture from the Bible? He is a gangsta! He curses! He's violent! Why would he call upon a verse of scripture addressing the crucifixion of Christ when many of his lyrics and personal choices seem ungodly? Is this a contradiction? Tricia Rose (1994) argued that Hip Hop deals with many complex social and cultural issues and at times can seem contradictory. She moves on to state that what seems contradictory are not necessarily signs of a lack of intellectual clarity. Rap music and rappers offer more than a single viewpoint, and

Rebel Music, pages 3–12

trying to understand these "poly-vocal" conversations that take place in music and videos out of context makes things seem irrational. Rappers such as Game and Lil Wayne struggle to make meaning of their lives and navigate rough terrain when it comes to performing what they feel are authentic interpretations/representations of being Black males and rappers in a music industry that is driven by the ideals of authenticity and street credibility.

In this chapter we discuss the complexity of Black life in America as well as how the views of Black males influence the performance of rappers and how it seems to guide their musical selections and choices. For this chapter, we will focus on the "My Life" (Taylor, 2008) song with Game and Lil Wayne and do a systematic analysis of the lyrical/thematic content of the song. This analysis will be done in light of the social locations of Black males in urban American society, and we will discuss issues of struggle, hope, love, and many other themes that occur throughout the song. We hope to provide a chapter that will spark critical discussion about many of the themes often overlooked and discarded when considering the value of rap songs by certain artists... in this case, Game and Weezy.

HIP HOP

Over 40 years ago on August 11, 1973, at 1520 Sedgwick Avenue, Clive Campbell (DJ Kool Herc), the father of Hip Hop, threw a party that has famously become known in Hip Hop circles as the birthday of the culture as we know it. Hip Hop has musical, linguistic, and cultural roots that go beyond the United States and was born out of a state of struggle during a time of economic and social ruin. The suffering South Bronx in the 1970s provided the environment for the creation of Hip Hop culture (Clay, 2003; Rose, 1994). The Bronx was a vivid example of the destruction caused by failed urban policy, structural racism, and faulty economic programs. Life for young Black and Latino youth residing in the Bronx was filled with daily struggles. These youth suffered in a city with staggering youth unemployment rates, with poor educational structures, and over-policed communities (Chang, 2005). Without stable employment or hope, youth generated Hip Hop to provide a sense of self-empowerment and to oppose the institutions and individuals responsible for their quality of life in these urban centers. Participation in Hip Hop culture provided a sense of community and social support for these often marginalized communities. Since that time, Hip Hop has grown from mainly serving as a voice for the marginalized and underserved Black and Latino residents of New York City to a worldwide multi-million dollar industry being used by the masses across the globe. However, this hyper-commodification of Black cultural expression has narrowed the presentation of the culture to a point where the industry is flooded with music and images that executives see as being financially viable in a corporately-driven market. Talent and quality of the message take a backseat to the marketing potential of the culture. Unlike in its early foundational days when Hip Hop was aligned with the cultural practices produced by Black urban youth, Hip Hop is now more representative of the ideals constructed by corporate leaders, who use Hip Hop to market their products and services to youth across the globe (Petchauer, 2009).

Even with the commercialization of the culture, it is still important to understand how youth perceive and participate in the culture. We must understand what youth bring to and take away from their devotion to Hip Hop cultural practices. Rap is often blamed for youth violence, the rise of gangs, drug use, and violence against women because of the prevalence of some "commercialized" rap lyrics that contain violent and misogynistic messages (Dixon & Brooks, 2002; Reyna, Brandt, & Viki, 2009). In this simplistic analysis, critics fail to acknowledge unjust social policies and institutional practices that aid in creating environments of violence in underserved communities. In addition, America's infatuation with violence in other forms of media is often overlooked outside of Hip Hop (Richardson & Scott, 2002). Violent material is aggressively marketed to youth through video games, movies, and music. This violence is not exclusive to Hip Hop culture, but is part of the larger American culture of violence. Hip Hop culture has been heavily influenced by an American theme of capitalism and other outside forces, but it also serves as a space where youth struggle with what it means to be raced, classed, and gendered individuals in a capitalistic, race-based society. Hip Hop allows youth to create knowledge and realize that their funds of understanding and lived realities are valued (Sawyer, 2013). A greater understanding of youth perspectives on Hip Hop, as well as other topics, can aid in developing an increased focus on issues and concerns that positively impact the lives of youth.

LIFE ACCORDING TO THE GAME AND LIL WAYNE

> Dear Lord, you done took so many of my people I'm just wonderin' why
> You haven't taken my life
> Like what the hell am I doing right. (Taylor, 2008)

In "My Life" by the Game and Lil Wayne (Taylor, 2008), the song begins with a powerful focus on urban struggle from Lil Wayne expressing his desire to stay "grindin" and pushing forward despite his lived realities. For some, witnessing such hope from a person facing these circumstances seems to be at odds with the nature of the social location of the individual. How can one still find hope in a state of existence that should produce hopelessness?

When we take a glance at current research on the plight of Black males in urban settings, national assessments and numerous articles consistently report that Black adolescent males are performing lower than other groups (Ladson-Billings, 2006; Noguera, 2008). It is also well documented that Black adolescent males are disproportionately placed in special education, school suspensions, and expulsions and are leading in school dropout rates, unemployment, and juvenile incarceration (Artiles & Trent, 1994; Artiles, 2003; Holzman, 2006). Duncan (2002) argues that Black males suffer a condition characteristic of a population that is beyond love. This is

> a condition of those who are excluded from society's economy and networks of care and thus expelled from useful participation in social life...black males are constructed as a strange population...as a group with values and attitudes that are fundamentally different from other students, their marginalization and oppression are understood as natural and primarily of their own doing. (p. 140)

He argues further that Black males are relatively powerless to define their circumstances and as a result are often relegated to a state of being defined by others. However, despite all of these descriptions, rather than give up, Lil Wayne paints the picture of an urban soldier that is pushing forward and looking for strength to make it from day to day. In this environment where drugs and death surround people living in urban communities, he still feels there is a reason to keep living despite the death that surrounds him. "Dear Lord, you done took so many of my people I'm just wonderin' why you haven't taken my life. Like what the hell am I doing right?" (Taylor, 2008). He doesn't understand why he is still alive, but he still shows resilience. One could assume that he is voicing frustration and wants to give up, but his questioning can also be seen as a cry for help...an attempt to understand his life and purpose. Everyone around him is dying, but for some reason, death misses him. What is his purpose for being alive? This common experience of death in urban areas has an impact on the psyche of those living in these urban spaces. Youth continue to struggle with an everyday living where avoiding danger is a regularly occurring feat. To be young, a youth of color, living in an urban environment means daily navigation of obstacles to avoid harm and in the worse case death.

> Take me away from the hood like a state penitentiary
> Take me away from the hood in the casket or a Bentley
> Take me away like I overdosed on cocaine
> Or take me away like a bullet from Kurt Cobain. (Taylor, 2008)

In the above verse, the Game articulates his frustration with his 'hood by voicing a desire to be removed from the environment. In addition, he highlights the conflicting romanticized relationship between young Black men and the 'hood. On one hand, there is a cry to escape from the place that serves as a metaphorical grave site for loved ones, plagued with misery, crime and death, yet there is an irony in the reference of the penitentiary, casket, drugs and the bullet as his rescuers. One might imply the Game is using sarcasm to symbolize the ever present social obstacles and lived experiences that define underserved urban spaces. More importantly, there is a romanticizing of prison, death, and drugs inherent in modern commercialized rap lyrics that foster an intimate connection between youth and these destructive factors. A sense of nihilism is produced as a result of negative images created through corporatized ideals of authentic Blackness in addition to existing in neighborhoods failed by faulty urban policy that in a way forces youth to find refuge in the worst alternatives to reality. Their desperation in trying to rationalize their everyday nightmare gives rise to acceptance of solutions that they have little control over to attain a desired outcome... "a way through the day" and a new reality.

It is important to note that the drastic measures he suggests (state penitentiary, casket, Bentley, or bullet) paints the picture of an individual reaching the end/edge of his sanity. He expresses a desire to get away from the 'hood by any means necessary, and his desire to leave the 'hood or earth should not be necessarily taken in a literal sense. His crying out for help is in line with what Kelley (2002) terms the Black radical imagination. This imagination allows people to live through their minds in "another space" and see life as possibility even if they are surrounded by desolation. There is this desire to strive for a better place. This imagination is what can give hope when all else is lost. It has to be better or, as Jay-Z said, "This can't be life." The idea of seeing a way out can be traced back to old negro spirituals when the enslaved Africans sung about getting beyond this land... not just mentally, but also striving for a physical manifestation of freedom from enslavement and other forms of oppression. A more modern "spiritual" that exhibits this notion of getting out is "Spaceship" by Kanye West when he expresses his desire to find a spaceship and fly away. Game is not asking for a spaceship to fly away or a chariot to swing low; he is, however, imagining a way to get from the violent reality of his everyday existence in his 'hood.

His call for a better life away from the 'hood is a realistic call when thinking of failed urban policies. It is often stated that education is the great equalizer, but for those living in the situation described by the Game and Lil Wayne, this is not the case. Schools have continuously failed students residing in urban spaces, thus having a negative impact on their life's trajectory. There is increasing correlation between Black males who are failed by the school system—and perform poorly—and eventually drop out, and their involvement with the penal system (Howard, 2008). Black males outnumber all other ethnic groups in the prison population and have a rate of incarceration five times higher than that of white males. One in every eight Black men in their twenties and thirties was behind bars in 2003 (Elsner, 2004 as referenced in Howard, 2008). Even scarier, Department of Justice statisticians project that based on current demographics, one in every three African-American men can expect to spend some time incarcerated, on probation, or under some type of jurisdiction of the penal system during his life time (Howard, 2008).

The lived experiences of Black males have often been characterized with a perceived lack of academic and personal motivation. Some even go as far to blame Hip Hop culture for this perceived lack of intellectual striving (McWhorter 2000, 2008). They point to a decrease in recreational reading among Black youth with an increase in listening to rap music and participation in Hip Hop culture and relate it to the fostering of a culture of anti-intellectualism. Their simplistic analysis is problematic, and the picture painted in "My Life" counteracts the notion that people want to live in rough environments and do not want to have better for themselves and their family. Trying to understand Hip Hop and the messages sent via rap songs out of context reduces our understanding to a one-side deficit driven understanding of young people and Hip Hop culture. Yes, there are many issues within the culture that need serious attention and possibly correction, but Hip Hop cannot be the blame for the social dysfunction that is a result of larger systems of privilege and oppression in our society. Using urban youth culture and Hip Hop as scapegoats removes the focus from an educational and social system that has repeatedly failed students, with a higher concentration of this failure residing in our urban centers (Anyon 1997; Kozol 1991, 2005; Oakes 1985).

In Game's first full verse, he highlights a parallel between one of Hip Hop's most notable emcees, Notorious B.I.G., and one of religion's most notable saviors, Jesus Christ. Christ is both "sacrificial lamb and vulnerable martyr and yet also an all-powerful being; he takes on the role of the reviled, threatened and murdered" (Perry, 2004, p. 148). Hip Hop, in many ways, has taken the role of spiritual force and the iconic rappers have become the "all-powerful beings" of the new "religious-less" generation. Biggie, both threatened and martyred, served as the voice of the 'hood and the most debased of society. Similarly, Christ was known for keeping the company of the sinners, the downtrodden, and outcasts. In a similar way, Biggie's lyrics attempted to rationalize the experiences of the forgotten people of the streets. Game goes further to compare himself with Christ as an "equal, [and] hated on so much" (Taylor, 2008). The association of rapper with savior gives rise to the notion that Hip Hop is the gospel of the people and rappers are their deliverers from evil. Both financially and spiritually rap has served as a vocal escape for the mind and a perceived viable financial escape from poverty.

As Hip Hop replaces religiosity for many youth, it can also be argued that rappers now serve as replacements for the father figure in the lives of urban youth. Hip Hop serves as a space for young urban men, particularly Black and Latino, to negotiate ideas and ideals of masculinity. In the line "like I needed my father, but he needed a needle" (Taylor, 2008), Game reveals the absence of his father, often a pandemic in the 'hood. Thus Game, rapper and voice of the youth, puts on the hat of "leader" for the young male. Instead of the father, rappers become the role models and shapers of young men. Unfortunately, because of the mass mediated images of perceive masculinity, it gets defined by the "gangsta" trope, glorifying destructive and violent behavior as the rites of passage for young males. Through these one-sided depictions, Hip Hop can be seen as a hyper-masculine genre authenticating masculinity through lyrical murals of violence, misogyny, and survival.

> And I ain't no preacher, but here's my Eric Sermon
> So eat this Black music and tell me how it taste now
> And fuck Jessie Jackson cause it ain't about race now. (Taylor, 2008)

Tricia Rose (2008) argued that Hip Hop would be the way in which we negotiated race in the 21st century. In the second verse, the Game references a cultural/age chasm that exists between the Civil Rights Movement and today's Hip Hop and post-Hip Hop generations. Todd Boyd (2002) also addressed this intergenerational gap in his book *The New H.N.I.C.: The Death of Civil Rights and the Reign of Hip Hop*. Boyd analyzes the differences and misunderstandings that arise between the groups. He argues that for modern youth, the methods of past generations cannot work in the current times. For him, the Civil Rights Movement is history, and Hip Hop is what will guide the ideas of protest and struggle for the current and future generations. In a similar way, Game makes a clear distinction between the leaders of the Civil Rights Movement and the poetic Hip Hop sermons that now "move the crowd." Hip Hop is the voice of the youth and, more importantly, it gives voice to the 'hood. Whereas the Black church served as the catalyst for Black political protest during the 1960s, Hip Hop takes the place of the non-violent marches and sit-ins led by Dr. King and a multitude of others, and in turn aggressively thrusts the harsh reality of the current struggles to the forefront. Game's aggressive quip to "eat this Black music" reveals a modern form of protest, very different from the boycotts of the sixties, and is reflected in his message referencing Jessie Jackson. Both generations have faced struggles but on different levels. The issues have evolved as well as the methods used to face/fight injustices. For the Game, Hip Hop is not trying to march about issues of race. Unfortunately, Game's statement, "It ain't about race now," can be misleading. Hip Hop has brought many races together, and some rappers have argued that it has done more for race relations than the Civil Rights Movement. This can be debated. However, although race is not the only issue, it is still a major issue. The picture that the Game paints about his neighborhood and other urban centers has plenty to do with racialized policies and a racial and economic hierarchy maintained by a system of racial privilege.

> Ain't no bars, but niggas can't escape the hood
> They took so many of my niggas, that I should hate the hood
> But it's real niggas like me that make the hood. (Taylor, 2008)

In closing, Game exhibits a love-hate relationship with his 'hood and the life that results from living in this urban space. On one hand, he hates the condition that he and his people are subjected to exist in, but on the other hand, he understands that his environment is what made him into the person he is today. Even with all of the problems and struggles in his 'hood, for him, he sees it as a foundational space that he is forever connected to, and forgetting this place would be like removing a part of who he is and this "'hood experience" is what keeps him grounded and seen as credible to the people residing there as well as his millions of rap fans.

In order for us to understand "My Life" and other songs, we have to take a step back and understand the nature of the music in the context of the larger American society. Trying to understand Hip Hop without understanding the story of its creation and the nature of the environments that continue to produce it, Hip Hop doesn't make sense. It is the rich culture of seeming contradiction and nuance that allows Hip Hop to exist and be critiqued. This chapter was not written to free Hip Hop or the producers of the culture from criticism. This is just one analysis of many that could have been submitted on this one song. There are many areas of analysis that were left out and hopefully will be taken up in future works of this nature. Building relationships with youth in a Hip Hop world is important for us to bridge the generational divide. In addition, with the changing times, increases in technology, and student investment in popular culture, it is important for our understanding of Hip Hop and youth culture to be complicated and expanded. We have to build partnerships that allow those involved to build the skills of critical media literacy and analysis. In order to continue to engage with the increasing corporatized version of Hip Hop, it is a disservice to take everything in as a mindless consumer. Moreover, for urban youth, critical media literacy is vital in order to participate and survive in a world that has been transformed by digital technology and new media culture (Kellner & Share, 2007). Our relationships with young people surrounding Hip Hop culture, and in particular rap music, should be grounded in the practices of youth critical media literacy development, which aims to allow youth to analyze, evaluate, critique, and produce multiple modes of communication (electronic, print, visual, etc.) while having the ability to vocalize and showcase what matters in their worlds (Goodman, 2003). This understanding of youth as creators and equal developers of knowledge creates a space where the possibilities of unification to address many social issues are endless.

REFERENCES

Anyon, J. (1997). *Ghetto schooling: A political economy of urban educational reform.* New York, NY: Teachers College Press.

Artiles, A. J. (2003). Special education's changing identity: Paradoxes and dilemmas in views of culture and space. *Harvard Educational Review, 73*(2), 164–202.

Artiles, A. J., & Trent, S. C. (1994). Overrepresentation of minority students in special education: A continuing debate. *The Journal of Special Education, 27*(4), 410–437.

Boyd, T. (2002). *The new HNIC: The death of civil rights and the reign of hip hop.* New York, NY: New York University Press.

Chang, J. (2005). *Can't stop won't stop: A history of the hip hop generation.* New York, NY: St. Martin's Press.

Clay, A. (2003). Keepin' it real: Black youth, hip-hop culture, and black identity. *American Behavioral Scientist, 46,* 1346–1358.

Dixon, T. L., & Brooks, T. (2002). Rap music and rap audiences: Controversial themes, psychological effects and political resistance. *African American Research Perspectives, 8,* 106–116.

Duncan, G. A. (2002). Beyond love: A critical race ethnography of the schooling of adolescent Black males. *Equity & Excellence in Education, 35*(2), 131–143.

Goodman, S. (2003). *Teaching youth media: A critical guide to literacy, video production & social change.* New York, NY: Teachers College Press.

Holzman, M. (2006). *Public education and Black male students: The 2006 state report card.* Cambridge, MA: Schott Foundation for Public Education.

Howard, T. C. (2008). Who really cares? The disenfranchisement of African American males in preK–12 schools: A critical race theory perspective. *Teachers College Record, 110*(5), 954.

Kelley, R. D. G. (2002). *Freedom dreams: The Black radical imagination.* Boston, MA: Beacon Press.

Kellner, D., & Share, J. (2007). Critical media literacy is not an option. *Learning inquiry, 1*(1), 59–69.

Kozol, J. (1991). *Savage inequalities: Children in American schools.* New York, NY: Crown Publishing.

Kozol, J. (2005). *The shame of the nation: The restoration of apartheid schooling in America.* New York, NY: Crown Publishing.

Ladson-Billings, G. (2006). From the achievement gap to the education debt: Understanding achievement in U.S. schools. *Educational Researcher, 35*(7), 3–12.

McWhorter, J. H. (2000). *Losing the race: Self-sabotage in Black America.* New York, NY: The Free Press.

McWhorter, J. H. (2008). *All about the beat: Why hip-hop can't save Black America.* New York, NY: Gotham.

Noguera, P. A. (2008). *The trouble with Black boys: And other reflections on race, equity, and the future of public education.* San Francisco, CA: Jossey-Bass.

Oakes, J. (1985). *Keeping track: How schools structure inequality.* New Haven, CT: Yale University Press.

Perry, I. (2004). *Prophets of the hood: Politics and poetics in hip hop.* Durham, NC: Duke University Press.

Petchauer, E. (2009). Framing and reviewing hip-hop educational research. *Review of educational research, 79*(2), 946–978.

Reyna, C., Brandt, M., & Viki, G. T. (2009). Blame it on hip-hop: Anti-rap attitudes as a proxy for prejudice. *Group Processes & Intergroup Relations, 12*(3), 361–380.

Richardson, J. W., & Scott, K. A. (2002). Rap music and its violent progeny: America's culture of violence in context. *The Journal of Negro Education, 71*(3), 175–192.

Rose, T. (1994). *Black noise: Rap music and black culture in contemporary America.* Hanover, NH: Wesleyan Press.

Rose, T. (2008). *The hip hop wars: What we talk about when we talk about hip hop—and why it matters.* New York, NY: Basic Civitas Books.

Sawyer III, D. C. (2013). "I Ain't do nothing!": An analysis of the social and academic experiences of black males in a dismantled middle school. (Unpublished doctoral). Syracuse University, Syracuse.

Taylor, J. (2008). My life [Recorded by The Game, featuring Lil Wayne]. On *LAX* [CD]. Los Angeles, CA: Geffen Records.

CHAPTER 2

"PETROLEUM DISTILLATION" BY FIFTEEN

Zack Furness (for Chad Stocker)

Having spent the last 14 or so years playing in punk bands, I've heard people tell a million stories about their favorite bands, their first shows, their best (and worst) performances, and quite often, some variation of how punk rock shaped who they are as individuals. I could probably tell a lot of these same stories if I wasn't cursed with an insanely bad memory, and if I actually thought most of them were worth recalling in the first place!

There are, of course, a handful of events that left an imprint in my mind like the mark of a branding iron. One such instance was early in college, when I was reintroduced to punk rock and instantly excited by the prospects of exploring everything possible. I found tons of new music and record labels to check out, but at the time I was still generally turned off by the kinds of bands who just screamed and played music as fast and/or abrasively as possible. Interestingly, I came to realize that a lot of those bands were the ones singing about real issues and the kinds of topics that were becoming increasingly important to me as I had just started college and was getting interested in learning about things that were definitely not part of my education in high school. But while I liked the *idea* of punk bands that had something substantial (or simply angry) to say about what was going

Rebel Music, pages 13–18

on in the world, a lot of their music just didn't do it for me. Fortunately, my best friend introduced me to his roommate, Chad, who convinced me that if I liked catchy punk songs, then I was crazy for not listening to more bands from the East Bay scene in Berkeley, California—the home of Green Day, as well as many other great punk acts that were mostly new to me. In particular, he told me that I *absolutely needed* to check out the band Fifteen. And so I did. And it was one of the pivotal moments in my punk autobiography.

Fifteen was the first band that really showed me that it was possible to combine melodic songs with an actual message—a way of genuinely "mixing pop and politics," as musician Billy Bragg once put it. They had a huge influence on me musically and lyrically, but especially politically. Because like so many of my favorite bands, writers, and teachers, Fifteen helped me to see politics as something that wasn't disconnected from my life, or as this painfully alienating set of things done exclusively by elderly government officials, faceless organizations, and the kinds of boring politicians that you see talking on C-Span when you flip past the TV channel on the way to something better. Instead, politics were presented as something rooted in participation, everyday life, art, community, and, most fundamentally, the idea of simply giving a shit about other people and the world in which we live. The band had a number of songs that drew clear links between what we might typically think of as "the personal" and "the political," but probably the best example I can think of is their song "Petroleum Distillation," which is the first track on their second record, *The Choice of a New Generation.*

From an outside perspective, writing a song called "Petroleum Distillation" and using punk music to call attention to problems as wide ranging as air pollution and drug abuse might seem rather striking, particularly when most people tend to think that punk was (or is) just about Mohawks, tattoos, or a form of rebellious angst limited to one's teenage years. While some bands do fit this description, Fifteen is part of a lineage of punk in which young people educate themselves about politics and are much more interested in talking about real issues than they are in trying to simply shock people with middle fingers and weird haircuts (neither of which are all that shocking nowadays). Like people in various punk scenes throughout the U.S. and countries throughout the world, Fifteen participated in benefit shows for progressive causes, tried to raise awareness about punks' failure to put their ethics into action, and idealistically called for people to change both the world and themselves.

"Petroleum Distillation" starts off with a super catchy bass line that forms the melody of the song, and it's important to mention this up front because people sometimes talk about the relevance of punk songs as if the only thing that really matters are the lyrics. Nothing could be further from the truth because there are plenty of things that you can hear someone say on a microphone or on a record, but it's the ability of a musician to combine ideas with a good song that actually gets people to *listen* to what's being said, instead of simply hearing it. Any true fan of punk or Hip Hop will tell you as much, regardless of how one defines a "good" song or expresses that sentiment. My point here is that even if you (the reader) and I have very different tastes in music, we can't think about the significance of songs by pulling lyrics apart from their music. In the same way, we can't really learn anything significant about a piece of music by extracting it from the larger social, cultural, and political contexts in which it was written, performed, purchased, remixed, or covered by a different artist—it's like trying to learn something interesting about a person without knowing where she's from, how she spends her time, what her family is like, and what kinds of things make her curious, passionate, depressed, or delighted.

With that being said, I want to talk about the lyrics to "Petroleum Distillation" because I think the song not only brings up important environmental and social issues, it also offers a unique point of entry for thinking about how people make sense of concepts like oppression and freedom, which are, after all, pretty difficult to contemplate without reference to each other—"oppression" is a vague concept if we don't have a baseline idea of what "freedom" means, and vice versa. By connecting the dots between some of the personal and social meanings of oppression and freedom, the song radically challenges conventional wisdom at the heart of American society and simultaneously provides a very basic introduction to some of the environmentalist and anarchist ideals that garnered support in various punk scenes from the late 1970s through the present day. More broadly, the lyrics offer a radical critique of capitalism by questioning some of it basic tenets (i.e., private property) as well as the everyday activities (i.e., driving cars) that are normalized or made part of our collective "common sense" in a capitalist society. Not everyone will agree with Fifteen's positions, but one doesn't necessarily have to agree with or even like a songwriter in order to try and understand what the artist is saying and why he or she is saying it.

In order to "unpack" the ideas expressed in the lyrics and further explain what they mean, it is useful to look at three intersecting themes that I see as the most prominent in the song: 1) capitalism as the oppression of humanity; 2) pollution as humanity's oppression of the Earth; and 3) autonomy as freedom from oppression. Before I elaborate and begin to dissect the lyrics in a way that is useful for my purposes, I think it is crucial to first get a clear sense of how the song actually sounds and feels. The best way to do this is by listening to the tune from start to finish (the original recording is posted on YouTube) while reading through the lyrics in the order in which they are sung.

CAPITALISM AS THE OPPRESSION OF HUMANITY

There are several things that really stick out when you listen to "Petroleum Distillation," and arguably the most prominent is the singer's raspy repetition of the chorus: "I know, I know, I know, I know that life has become slavery" (Ott, 1994). When Jeff Ott—the singer/guitarist/songwriter in Fifteen—invokes the institution of slavery in this song, he's really doing two things at once. First, in the most general sense he's using slavery as a metaphor to describe how we're all basically tethered to a way of life that doesn't necessarily make sense ("a little too easy seems a little too hard today") and is oftentimes harmful to ourselves and others in ways that we not tend to easily comprehend. But the song also uses slavery as an analogy for the social conventions and laws that quite literally deny us the ability choose the kinds of lives that we want to live. The message is not that capitalism turns us into slaves who have to wear shackles, have no freewill, or experience the kind of dehumanizing, institutionalized violence doled out to Black and Indigenous peoples throughout much of U.S. history. Rather, the lyrics ask us to think about how the interrelated institutions of work, rent, and private property serve as invisible shackles that inhibit our ability to make truly free choices and, by extension, our ability to live as free people.

When Ott sings the lines "paying money for four walls leaves the slavery intact" and "it's against the law to sleep on the ground in God's land" (Ott, 1994), he's calling attention to the fact that, first and foremost, people are forced to work in order to pay for housing, regardless of whether they love or hate their jobs. This seems like a very normal proposition to most people, and it is normal so long as we don't consider housing a human right or, for example, that people lived for thousands of years on this continent (and throughout much of the world) without adhering to the "normal" idea of being forced to work for a wage in order pay money for shelter. Most of us willingly comply with this arrangement, and we may not even think twice about the dominant ideology, or worldview, that justifies the arrangement itself. But the important part to recognize here is that we don't actually have the ability to "opt out" of this system if we don't like it. That is to say, the threat of criminal punishment and/or imprisonment ensures nearly universal compliance (this is the less invisible part of our "invisible shackles"). For example, if someone becomes unemployed or simply wants to spend the majority of his time on activities that do not earn a paycheck—such as raising children, doing volunteer work, practicing music, or making art—then he will eventually get evicted for not paying rent and he will end up homeless. If someone becomes homeless—as was the case with Fifteen's singer, who was homeless for years in Berkeley, California—that person becomes a criminal by default since there are laws in nearly every U.S. city that make it illegal for people to sleep, hang out (loitering), and in some cases even sit or lie down (sit/

lie ordinances) in public spaces as well as on private property (trespassing). Once a person has a criminal record, it becomes incredibly difficult to find a job or a place to live; and if one gets enough criminal violations, then one can also be locked up in prison, which is the ultimate way of denying a person his or her freedom (and often forcing one to do unpaid work that is, for all intents and purposes, a form of slave labor).

Long story short: this song is part of a much longer history of political critique that argues that we are free in a capitalist society only to the extent that we do what we're told and we don't question the cultural norms, social institutions, or laws that "leave the slavery intact."

POLLUTION AS HUMANITY'S OPPRESSION OF THE EARTH

Any punk song named after the process of refining oil clearly has a message about the environment, and "Petroleum Distillation" points to some of the specific as well as the general ways in which human beings oppress the natural world. In addition to beginning the first verse by talking about fossil fuel emissions ("the clouds arising from the cars we drive"), Ott tallies a list of pollutants that negatively impact the environment including lead, toxic waste, fluorocarbons, and petroleum distillates. Instead of just simply pointing the finger elsewhere, the lyrics make it clear that Fifteen is self-reflective about everyone's role in the ecological problems they're addressing, including the band itself; for example, they use possessive pronouns to talk about "the cars *we* drive," or to note that "*we're* all one sick race" (Ott, 1994, italics added). They make it clear that the political problem of environmental pollution is also a very personal issue, and the lyrics in the second to last verse draw explicit comparisons between the act of abusing oneself (particularly with drugs) and abusing the Earth: "The water's my heart, it's been broken with booze and drugs and shooting up paste [heroin]" (Ott, 1994). Seeing such problems in this way make it possible for anyone to relate to one of the lines that repeats in slight variations throughout the song: "I'm afraid my children are going to have to watch the world waste away." Indeed, one of the song's strong points in this regard is how they simultaneously point to various levels of connection that exist within the environment (the links between the ground, sky, water, and sun), as well as between people and the Earth (spiritually and biologically), and also between human's industrial byproducts and natural ecosystems.

AUTONOMY AS FREEDOM FROM OPPRESSION

With all the criticisms that this song makes about capitalism, organized religion ("Costs two dollars a minute and additional charges to pray to God today"), environmental destruction, and even drug abuse, one could easily assume that Fifteen is cynical about the ability for people to create substantial changes in society. But the last verse actually offers a really positive vision for imagining a different world, and it begins with the assertion that "autonomy shall reward itself with freedom" (Ott, 1994). Autonomy is a concept that essentially describes freewill and agency, which is a way of thinking about individuals living their lives independently and making decisions based on their freewill, without coercion. Anarchism, which is a political philosophy based on the idea that people are capable of governing themselves without leaders or hierarchies, is one of many political paradigms that recognizes that the functioning of a free society relies on people having a healthy amount of autonomy. Fifteen is clearly indebted to this line of thinking, and like many other anarchists, socialists, and libertarians, they also recognize that a free society is one in which people collectively create the conditions in which *everyone* can enjoy autonomy. In other words, this isn't an argument for people to just "do their own thing"; it is a way of seeing freedom as something that challenges oppression on all fronts, whether that oppression comes from the State, from powerful corporations, or from a mindset that promotes the domination of people or the environment. As part of this collective vision of freedom, the band not only argues that humility is a path toward peace, they also suggest that we can all come together ("the integration of humanity") if we are able get beyond the desire for material things ("the dissolution of possession") and realize our true obligations to "our lives and our Earth" (Ott, 1994). The last part is crucial inasmuch as the song reminds us that we need to be mutually responsible for our own collective liberation and for how we treat the planet that sustains all life.

REFERENCE

Ott, J. (1994). Petroleum distillation [Recorded by Fifteen]. On *Choice of a new generation* [CD]. Berkeley, CA: Lookout Records.

PART II

MARGINALIZATION

CHAPTER 3

"LADIES FIRST" BY QUEEN LATIFAH

Noelle Chaddock

One of the conversations I remember being exposed to in graduate school was about the homogeneity of classical philosophy. It is important to note that philosophy has grown a lot in the last 50 years or so to include women and People of Color. However, the vast majority of philosophy, and what is often offered to students as philosophy, is dominated by white men. Most of what I was encountering in graduate school positioned white men as the authority on philosophy, and all other theories seemed to be an enhancement or challenge to classical philosophy. For many of my colleagues, some of whom were People of Color like me, philosophy was written from a predominantly white male perspective. Even when theory was focused on People of Color, it often lacked any resemblance to our lived experiences. Mostly, we just felt like we were not represented by, considered in, or a part of the philosophy to which we were exposed. The sense that philosophy was dominated by and intended to represent only white males led us to a conversation about finding the philosophical or theoretical voice of oppressed People of Color. This is an old and ongoing conversation in philosophy. In our case, we ended up with Hip Hop as a counter model to classical philosophy. We found Hip Hop to be philosophical, inclusive of all kinds of people,

Rebel Music, pages 21–27

and representative of many of our lived experiences. For me in particular, Hip Hop became a way to engage students in conversations about social and political (socio-political) philosophy and Black feminism.

If we understand philosophy as a study of existence, knowledge, and reality, then Hip Hop deserves consideration as a philosophical discourse or conversation. Yet, like many art forms that intersect philosophy, not all of Hip Hop *is* philosophy. But, for the Hip Hop that pursues questions of knowledge of reality rather than affirmations of a status quo, we can see how Hip Hop philosophers offer a different perspective from traditional philosophers. I am not suggesting that everyone and anyone is or can be a philosopher. But, what I offer students enrolled in my *Hip Hop Culture* course is the idea that there are Hip Hop artists doing philosophy and that this is a possibility for them as well. This framework has guided many of my students towards becoming philosophy majors and minors over the years, and they have been able to produce philosophy that makes sense to them, while also being exposed to the rich traditions of classical philosophy.

At its core, Hip Hop is a socio-political philosophy. Events of the late 1960s in and around the South Bronx set a cultural, social, and political shift into motion. An African American and Latino consciousness and understanding stimulated the birth of the music that we now know as Hip Hop. Not just a form of music, Hip Hop became a genre of performance symptomatic of the lives of urban youth of color. In that moment, Hip Hop offered a social and political perspective that was no longer white or upper class. For the first time, socio-political philosophy was produced by urban youth of color about urban youth of color. No longer just the subject of philosophy, Hip Hop artists were also philosophers.

Cultural critic Tricia Rose (2008) points to earlier Hip Hop artists like Public Enemy, Queen Latifah, and KRS-One as examples of the political basis of Hip Hop. In her opinion, the "legacy of justice-based lyrics and activism and community building" (Rose, 2008, p. 108) generates the core of Hip Hop's link to socio-political philosophy. Indeed, the storytelling components of Hip Hop, its lyrics that speak of economic depression and racial injustice, give support to the idea of Hip Hop as a philosophical discourse.

While many of the notable Hip Hop artists are male, we must pay special attention to the unique kind of socio-political philosophy produced by women of color. After spending time with Hip Hop as a socio-political philosophy, I came to realize that artists like Queen Latifah gave us a unique perspective through a Black feminist philosophy. Women of color who produce Hip Hop philosophy and Black feminism are not only responding to race and poverty; they are also responding to the male dominance and oppression within Hip Hop. This gives philosophers like Queen Latifah a very interesting position from which to think and generate theory.

Queen Latifah, born Dana Owens, credits her mother as the main influence in her life. In the biography *Queen Latifah: The Hidden Side of the Queen,* Daz Willingham says that "her mother was an especially important figure in her life" (Willingham, 2012, p. 22). Queen Latifah's mother, Rita Owens, was a school teacher, and her father, Lancelot Owens, was a police officer. When her parents divorced, Dana was only eight years old, yet her mother maintained a life of stability for her and her brother. Not unlike many women, particularly women of color, divorce was a one-way ticket to the projects for Rita Owens and her two children. Rita Owens worked two jobs, leaving her children in the care of relatives who renamed Dana as Latifah, meaning "gentle and kind" (Willingham, 2012, p. 29). Latifah added Queen to her name almost ten years later.

Latifah was an active student involved in sports and musical theatre. But while she was attracted to Hip Hop from the beginning, "Latifah couldn't relate to the misogyny in the genre, she couldn't see herself being a part of it" (Willingham, 2012, p. 29). Latifah started to participate in Hip Hop as a beat boxer, and by the time she graduated from high school, she had attracted the attention of MTV and Tommy Boy Records.

Queen Latifah's first album was titled *All Hail the Queen* and was released in 1989; this is the album from which her song and greatest contribution to Black feminist philosophy, "Ladies First," came. From the beginning of her career, Queen Latifah rapped with a Black feminist perspective that made "her anti-sexist anthems became popular among urban women" (Willingham, 2012, p. 37). As Queen Latifah was recognized by the Rock and Roll Hall of Fame, the Billboard Top 10, BET, the Golden Globes, the Oscars, *Rolling Stone,* and the Black Film Awards, among others, she never lost her roots in Black feminism. Queen Latifah continued to produce socio-political philosophy through the death of her brother, the creation of his foundation for underprivileged youth, and her next Grammy winning album *U.N.I.T.Y.*

Queen Latifah wrote her autobiography *Ladies First* in 1991 and a second book entitled *Put on Your Crown: Life-Changing Moments on the Path to Queendom* in 2010. Latifah also started a record label featuring major musicians like LL Cool J, Outkast, Naughty by Nature, and Monica. She has also had an active acting career spanning almost two decades in TV, film, and stage productions. Latifah's success, however, has not changed her focus on feminism. According to Willingham, Queen Latifah has "made her art into a platform that would restore dignity to women and help females to see themselves as more than physical objects" (Willingham, 2012, p. 8). When I think of Hip Hop philosophy, Queen Latifah is the first philosopher that comes to mind, and she was a big influence on my framework for teaching philosophy to the Hip Hop generation.

Hip Hop has provided me with a way to engage youth, in particular urban youth, in the discipline/study of philosophy without having to translate a philosophical work that was often dominated by a singular white perspective. Philosophy became accessible through the recognizable form of Hip Hop: my students had been exposed to philosophy without knowing it was philosophy. Students, regardless of their backgrounds, came to the classroom having consumed Hip Hop elsewhere and thus having some understanding of the language Hip Hop was written in. This language also often reflected the voice of many students' own lived experiences or experiences that students had been exposed to through media and music. The language of Hip Hop's urban youth spoke theory clearly and simply.

I took over my Hip Hop class in 2008 from a professor who had principally focused on analyzing lyrics and performance even though it was intended to be an examination of culture. As a child of 1980s bubble gum pop, I knew little about Hip Hop as a music consumer. But I gained a profound appreciation for the theoretical content in Hip Hop. Thus was born my version of Hip Hop philosophy. I was eager to get students excited about philosophy and critical race theory. The class moved very quickly from a class full of consumers interpreting lyrics to a class full of budding philosophers actively engaging the socio-political philosophy they found in Hip Hop. As a teacher, my love for Hip Hop grew as I realized how much philosophy was available in its varied types.

Students started to connect Hip Hop lyrics with the writings of "traditional philosophers" and produced some interesting examinations of these connections. This served to expose students to the study of philosophy, the writing of theory, and to critical race arguments about philosophy. Students also began to see themselves *as* future philosophers. They started to distinguish between Hip Hop artists that were doing philosophy and those intending to entertain. Students were also able to recognize those rappers who were doing conscious, critical work versus those that were contributing to, or perpetuating the oppression of urban youth and other oppressed people. What is striking is the number of students who become interested in and chose to major/minor in philosophy, critical race theory, feminism, women's studies, queer studies, Black feminism or Africana Studies because of their experience with Hip Hop philosophy. One of my female students found that she discovered for the first time that "philosophy and theory were for and about her too." Hip Hop and Hip Hop philosophy *are* points of access to Black feminism. Hip Hop is often condemned for its misogyny, homophobia, and objectification: inarguably Hip Hop has a lot of work to do in those areas. Yet Hip Hop also offers access to socio-political philosophy along with a tradition of self-criticism. We see someone like Queen Latifah producing both feminism and socio-political philosophy in a way that she might not have in another career path. While it is clear that Latifah was focused from the start on female empowerment and feminism, her ability to generate philosophy and have it understood by the young women she was trying to reach really only works in Hip Hop philosophy. Hip Hop produces philosophy that young listeners are open to, understand, and then reproduce. This allows the philosophical conversations about how women and LGBTQ folks are treated and talked about in Hip Hop to occur from the perspective of those living those identities.

What is truly compelling about Hip Hop's relationship to Black feminism is the way in which Black women are leading the philosophical conversation. Rather than Black women being the object of feminist observations, they are the creators of their own worldviews. Black feminist women are creating an independent space and discourse as Hip Hop artists while continuing to be a part of its economic and commercial structure. Rather than Black feminists breaking away from the male dominated realm of Hip Hop, they write and theorize from its interior.

I have not had a class in four years that rejected Queen Latifah's "Ladies First" as a Hip Hop classic or as a Black feminist text. Latifah's lyrics hold a particular place in my student's Hip Hop philosophical journey. "That's old school gold"... "She knew what she was saying"... "That's when rap was good." While students pay Latifah homage as a Hip Hop Hip Hop artist, they often come to realize that they are also celebrating a particular Black feminist moment. It is clear that Latifah herself intended "Ladies First" as the beginning of a Black feminist movement both in and against the male dominated Hip Hop machine.

Latifah establishes the power of women with certainty in lyrics such as "a woman can bear you break you take you" (Owens, 1989). She also acknowledges the work her sister rappers have done that continues to go unnoticed because they are women.

> Now it's time to rhyme can you relate to a sister dope enough to make you holler and scream... conversating to the folks that have no whatsoever clue... Pleased with all the beats and rhymes my sisters have employed... Let me state the position, ladies first, yes?... Yeah, there's going to be some changes in here. (Owens, 1989)

The conversation unleashed with "Ladies First" lights a fire in the hearts of the future feminists, theorists, and philosophers in my class. "Ladies First" helps my students realize Latifah as a feminist while fostering a sense of Hip Hop's potential as a philosophical medium. Hip Hop as philosophy is accessible to the students who are quickly able to accept the lyrics as theory and then realize the role of theory in a more general sense. The energy around realizing something *they* own as youth, especially my students from urban areas, is viable. Students very quickly put together the work of Tricia Rose, bell hooks, and Audre Lorde as part of the same conversation in Latifah's

"Ladies First." Students become willing to read more complex texts, and they can move back and forth between the lyrics and the more traditional theory.

Like feminists before her, Latifah lauds the talents and contributions of female rappers, but she is also pointing to larger issues of Black women in society, Black society specifically. Not only do I find the theoretical content of Hip Hop accessible, I find it relatable to the lives of my students. "Ladies First" gives us Black motherhood, a topic most of my students are interested in either through personal experience or through Hip Hop's regular focus on motherhood. Latifah rhymes:

> pay me every bit of your attention like mother, like daughter... Desperately stressing I'm the daughter of a sister who's the mother of a brother who's the brother of another Plus one more, all four have a job to do, we doing it Respect due, to the mother who's the root of it..." (Owens, 1989)

Students quickly connect the critical issues of motherhood across theoretical genres like feminism, sociology, philosophy, women's studies, and so on. But Latifah's work ignites a sense of urgency in my students to contribute to these conversations. When a student understands Latifah's lyrics as "right on," that creates an opportunity for me to introduce other theorists outside of Hip Hop examining similar ideas. This is where philosophy, in particular Black feminism, starts making sense in a relatable way for many of my students.

Hip Hop is philosophy and theory in the most raw and unmediated forms. Students can almost immediately digest and reproduce Hip Hop theory while, perhaps more importantly in terms of access, relating Hip Hop theory to other non-Hip Hop theoretical positions. The students in my Hip Hop philosophy class end up exploring sociology, anthropology, literature, performing arts, and philosophy by the end of our time with Latifah's work. "Ladies First" is an "aha!" moment for students as well as a call to arms for establishing necessary anti-misogynistic frameworks for future Hip Hop theory.

Students have expressed a sense that feminism is a way of life for Latifah and find something to hang on to there. This creates a want for more feminist writings and perspectives, which has led some students on an interdisciplinary journey in philosophy and other theoretical frameworks: a journey many of my students say started with Latifah's "Ladies First" as a Black feminist writing.

Despite the age of the actual song, there is an automatic connection for today's young women, especially women of color, to their sense of displacement and marginalization not only in Hip Hop but in many parts of their lived experiences. Their male counterparts really set the stage for Latifah's work to spark a revolution in the classroom. Male students often start our first days of class taunting their female counterparts that "girls can't rap" and that "the only place girls belong is in videos not on the mic." Introducing Latifah's work early in the semester changes the climate of the classroom to one of critical engagement, rather than a perpetuation of male dominance and marginalization of female students. Latifah demands male respect in her lyrics and her life: "believe me when I say being a woman is great, you see I know all the fellas out there will agree with me..." (Owens, 1989).

Women in Hip Hop challenge traditional philosophy as well as mainstream Hip Hop through their Black feminist theory. Latifah opened a door to critical engagement and performative expression that generated an accessible feminist discourse for a generation more inclined towards non-traditional ways of receiving and interpreting theory. As Latifah rhymed in 1989, my students still find her message salient today:

> some think that we can't flow stereotypes, they got to go I'm a mess around and flip the scene into reverse with what? With a little touch of ladies first who said the ladies couldn't make it, you must be blind if you don't believe, well here, listen to this rhyme *ladies first*... (Owens, 1989)

REFERENCES

Owens, D. (1989). Ladies first [Recorded by Queen Latifah]. On *All hail the queen* [CD]. New York, NY: Tommy Boy.

Rose, T. (2008). *The hip hop wars: What we talk about when we talk about hip hop and why it matters.* New York, NY: Basic Books.

Willingham, D. (2012). *Queen Latifah: The hidden side of the queen.* New York, NY: Queen Latifah Biography.

CHAPTER 4

"NAILING DESCARTES TO THE WALL" BY PROPAGANDHI

Lauren Corman
Sarat Colling

I think the "punk" scene is where I first encountered any ideas about animal liberation. I recall a lot of the early '80s UK political punk bands referring to things like the fur industry and animal experimentation in their songs. So that had an effect on me; discovering that there were concrete choices you could make if you had private doubts about human society's relationship with animals. I think that's all we aim for too in respect to being a band in a "punk" scene; encourage people's private doubts.

—Chris Hannah, 2012, personal correspondence

Lauren: Have you ever stumbled upon something that you didn't know you were searching for until you've found it? That was me with punk rock. I was sixteen, living in rural Manitoba, and badly itching to leave my small town. The progressive politics and instrumental aggression of the music offered a lifeline to radically different ways of thinking and being. Before I went to live shows, I spent hours in the basement poring over punk lyrics and looping tracks, trying to decipher their meanings and just relishing the noise.

Rebel Music, pages 29–39

Politics moved from the abstract to the concrete at my first Propagandhi show, a benefit concert for PAAL (People Acting for Animal Liberation), which was also my first foray into live punk, in 1995. It was a warm evening in Winnipeg, heat kicking off parking lots and prairie sky melting orange into blue. My friends and I downed some beef burritos at Taco Bell and stumbled into a sweaty throng of teenagers packed into the all-ages show. Information tables lined the walls. The crowd buzzed with adrenalin. As I tried to catch my bearings, I glanced right and my eyes met those of a terrified monkey. He was writhing in pain, his eyes frantic as an experimenter restrained him, his mouth stretched in an unbroken scream.

PAAL was playing an anti-vivisection video. (Vivisection is the practice of performing operations on live animals for scientific research.) Unable to sustain my gaze, I quickly looked away. Moments later, Propagandhi played, "Nailing Descartes to the Wall/(Liquid) Meat is Still Murder," from their now classic 1996 album *Less Talk, More Rock.* The connection between the monkey on the screen and the cow who had been my beef taco hit me, and in that instant, I became vegetarian.

Sarat: I first heard Propagandhi in 2006, as part of an interview on the animal rights and liberation radio show, Animal Voices. Lauren was talking with the lead singer, Chris Hannah. Two years prior, I had learned about animal liberation, which led me to become vegan (no animal products, from meat, dairy, or eggs; no wool and leather; and no animal tested products). My transformation was spurred by a simple but profound assertion along the lines of, "The person who purchases a fur coat is as responsible for the death and suffering of the animals as those who make and sell the coat, and those who do the killing." I had always loved animals, but growing up on a small island secluded from the terror of animal industries, I had never thought about how some of my consumer choices harm others. In the interview, Hannah made connections between human and animal liberation. He said that our society relies on unprecedented exploitation and that only a paradigm shift that values the environment and labor would make a difference for animals. After hearing the interview, I picked up the album *Less Talk, More Rock,* soon followed by the others.

Propagandhi quickly became the soundtrack to my expanding political consciousness and budding activism, which included distribution of Vegan Outreach pamphlets. When I found it hard to imagine approaching strangers and asking whether I could offer them information on how animals are raised for food, I'd pop in my ear buds and play one of Propagandhi's animal liberation tracks to get psyched. The band's uncompromising and unapologetic approach encouraged me to bring out these aspects in myself, and it made me a better activist.

INTRODUCTION

Many people consider Propagandhi to be a life-changing band. They give you an intellectual and emotional thrashing that holds you to account and offers no apologies, all while asking the same of themselves: personal and political responsibility to pay attention and to resist injustices that are often plainly hidden in front of us (in advertising, war propaganda, news media, etc.) and that are perpetuated by our actions. Their songs demand that we turn privilege on its head and consider life from a different point of view, one often marginalized, ridiculed, and critical of mainstream society. When we do, things start looking more corrupt and brutal than ever imaginable.

Perhaps no songs are more potent in this regard than the ones about animal exploitation. This stuff isn't easy to hear. Hannah (Animal Voices Radio, 2006) has remarked that their animal-focused songs have generated the most negative responses. Maybe that's because we're all implicated, often three times a day. (How could fluffy marshmallows or wiggly neon Jell-O really contain pigskin and cattle hooves? Like other products of the "animal industrial complex" [Noske, 1997], gelatin is a seemingly innocuous ingredient with a gruesome back-story.)

The focus of this chapter, "Nailing Descartes to the Wall/(Liquid) Meat is Still Murder," is a blistering minute-long wake up call, shaking us out of our delusions of happy animals frolicking on Old MacDonald's farm. The song is part of an album-long punk manifesto that powerfully articulates the band's ethical and political commitments, ones that laid the foundation for sixteen proceeding years of music; each *Less Talk, More Rock* CD or record is marked with an anarchist circle-A, surrounded by the words, "Pro-feminist, animal-friendly, gay-positive, anti-fascist." As reflected in the album art, animal ethics have always been included within, and indivisible from, Propagandhi's larger political and ethical concerns. Below we break down the lyrics and give them some additional context. Throughout, we draw on an interview we recently did with Hannah about the song.

THE FATHER OF MODERN PHILOSOPHY MEETS HIS END

The Title: "Nailing Descartes to the Wall"

Propagandhi has a knack for describing scenarios that "turn the tables" on humans by imagining us as victims of the same violence we routinely inflict on other animals. Even the title of this song points to such turning: Descartes is nailed to the wall, not animals (his regular test subjects). Descartes was an influential seventeenth century philosopher, mathematician, and scientist who theorized the separation between mind and body. You've probably heard his statement, "I think; therefore I am." While often celebrated by Western science, his philosophy, known today as Cartesianism, proved most unfortunate for animals.

Descartes believed that humans are the only living beings with souls. According to him, because animals lack a soul, then they must lack consciousness. Although they have a brain, thus the biological "infrastructure" to receive images of the world (an apple, a tree, etc.), without a soul to receive the sense input, animals cannot be aware of, or think about, their surroundings (Kazes, 2010, p. 25). For instance, a cat will often respond with excitement to a bird flying outside the window, chattering and fixating on her movements. Rather than this being a conscious experience, Descartes would say that because the cat lacks a soul to receive the "image" of the bird, she is simply reacting like a machine.

Just as one would disassemble a machine to examine its components, Descartes and his contemporaries pulled apart living animals to examine their bodies. They cut open animals to observe their beating hearts, and they burnt, mutilated, and beat them, among other tortures. One eyewitness observed that the Cartesians "nailed the poor animals to boards by four paws to dissect them while still alive, in order to watch the circulation of the blood" (Fontaine, as quoted in Rupke, 1990, p. 27).

DOING NOTHING STILL DOES SOMETHING

> Stop consuming animals.
>
> I speak outside what is recognized as the border between reason and insanity. But I consider it a measure of my humanity to be written off by the living graves of a billion murdered lives. (Hannah, 1996)

Hannah shifts from request ("Consider someone else") to demand ("Stop consuming animals") through a spoken word one-two-punch that bridges the end of "Apparently I'm a PC Fascist" and the start of "Nailing Descartes to the Wall." That we might contemplate the lives of those we eat, and that such awareness should prompt us to stop eating them, remains controversial. The assertion that animal products were once "someone" can seem radical despite the fact that, on some level, we know animals aren't really walking pork chops or faceless steaks that skip to slaughter.

Yet social and economic forces conspire to make us to believe that we're not eating some*ones* (animals and substances from their bodies) but some*things* (meat, dairy, and eggs). In this way, these first few lyrics are quintessential punk: A willingness to question the mainstream and entertain a different point of view, regardless of its popularity. Skeptical? Try this: Next time you're eating at a typical North American home, declare that killing animals constitutes murder and that your friends are dining on corpses, and see how long it takes before the mashed potatoes hit the fan and people awkwardly excuse themselves from the table.

Despite the raised eyebrows, ridicule, and outright hostility sometimes directed toward animal activists, as the song suggests, these responses can actually affirm our solidarity with other animals rather than inspire self-doubt. A refusal to allow our bodies to serve as living graves reflects positively on us as critical thinkers and compassionate people.

Punk can be a great inoculation against society's oppressive status quo. At its best, punk makes us feel less alone and helps us resist when we encounter a disconnect between what we're told is normal and what we feel is right. The sense of disjuncture can happen at a very young age, as is often the case with animal issues. In various interviews, Hannah alludes to a hunting trip he went on when he was six. As he explained to us,

> It was one of my first memories of feeling like I was from another planet. . . . As some perceived male rite of passage in a tiny rural community where hunting and trapping were normal pastimes, I was sent out on a hunting trip with the neighborhood dads and made to carry the body of a beautiful drake mallard they had blasted out of the sky back to town on my lap in the back of the car. I remember the adults laughing and nudging each other as I sat there with this creature, feeling the warmth drain from her body and wondering what the point of all this could possibly be. (Hannah, personal communication, August 1, 2012)

Decades later, he's still wondering. Over and over again, we see that the harshest of treatment is meted upon those most deserving of mercy. We routinely take what's most precious to others (their lives), and often for incredibly trivial reasons.

WHY PEOPLE ARE PISSED OFF

> And I'm not ashamed of my recurring dreams about me and a gun and a different species [hint: starts with "h" and rhymes with "Neuman's"] of carnage strewn about the stockyards, the factories and farms. (Hannah, 1996)

The phrase "It's just an animal" dismisses the significance of animals' lives. The shorthand snuffs out the conversation and minimizes concern, sweeping it away in one rhetorical brush stroke, as if the very fact that they're animals somehow explains their treatment. On some level, it seems outrageous to suggest that animals matter enough to inspire vengeance. There's a widespread notion that animals don't think as much, or feel as much, as human beings, and that there's some major fundamental difference between us that justifies their large-scale use and harm. Yet Hannah's description of revenge starts to make metaphorical sense when we consider that pigs, for example, are extremely friendly, playful, and intelligent. Animals are just as feeling and desiring of their lives as we are, but we don't get much of an opportunity to know their personalities.

Although a staggering 696 million land animals are killed every year for food in Canada (over eight billion in the United States, and over 56 billion globally), farm animals are strangely absent from most North Americans' lives and remain largely erased from countrysides: As the demand for meat and other animal products has grown, so has the industrialization and intensification of farming practices. Instead of overrunning pastures, most so-called "food animals" now spend the bulk of their bleak lives in windowless buildings where they are fattened for slaughter or used to produce milk and eggs.

Animal products are in everything from roads (used in concrete) to books (used in binding glues). Animals are such a major part of the daily functioning of our economies and societies that their commodification and consumption seems natural. Many of us don't question the origins of the meat and dairy we eat, or wonder about the animal testing involved in most shampoo and other products. We often know (and ask) even less about the perspectives of those whose lives and deaths made these products possible, yet many wouldn't allow our cats or dogs to be treated with the cruelty shown to so-called farm or lab animals.

Maybe the dream described in this song doesn't seem so extreme when our myths about animals unravel. We'd be desperate to stop the suffering of loved ones in similar conditions. Imagining humans as victims of the horror we inflict on animals challenges us to question our ethical double standard. It begs the question, why is the song at its most controversial when we realize that the "different species" under attack is actually ours?

THE OPEN SECRET

> Still I know as well as anyone that it does less good than harm to be this honest with a conscience eased by lies. (Hannah, 1996)

Is awareness about the treatment of animals on factory farms enough to inspire people to change? Perhaps our ideologies are so entrenched that these conditions seem acceptable, and our taste for animal products is so habitualized that we're afraid to change. Or perhaps we are so distanced from these conditions we forget the violence. Maybe the apparatuses that perpetuate animal exploitation are ultimately sustained by the lies we tell ourselves. Our willed ignorance. Professor Una Chauduri argues,

> our relationship to animals is kind of the great open secret of our society and culture. Anthropologists have this theory about how cultures are often organized around certain things that you know not to know. . . . You are aware of something, but you do not acknowledge that you are aware of it. (Bryant, Chaudhuri, Jamieson, Moore, & Wolfson, 2006, p. 33)

The lies about animals are many, and stereotypes about pigs, in particular, abound: They're filthy. They're lazy gluttons. Even their names signal negative attributes: "Hog" means taking more than one's fair share, while "pig" signifies both power-hungry cops and capitalists. Call someone "swine," and see how she responds! Empathy with those who are vilified can feel risky, but then again, so is knowing and not acting on what we know.

Guilt is one of the worst feelings, and we do almost anything to avoid it. The functioning of industrial agriculture rests on our willingness to tell ourselves stories about who animals are, and how they're treated (e.g., "I love animals, but people need to eat meat in order to be healthy"). Guilt can trigger knee-jerk reactions and make us recoil or lash out as our stories' veneers are punctured. Sometimes we might just feel powerless to have any real positive impact. When you consider that the average U.S. American meat eater will consume about two thousand animals, veganism (not to mention your impact on people around you) can help a lot. If you don't know where to start, check out some of the resources at the end of this chapter. For example, Hannah suggests that everyone watch the documentary, *Earthlings* (Monson, 2005).

CRIMES AGAINST ANIMALS

> But you cannot deny that meat is still murder. Dairy is still rape. (Hannah, 1996)

Usually, humans are the only species considered victims of murder or rape, if they are considered victims at all. For example, if someone shoots and kills both a human and their dog, the killer may face an animal cruelty charge, but a murder charge applies only to the human death. This double standard stems from the idea that humans are special because supposedly we are the only animals with capacities such as language and reason. (Of course, this sentiment also ignores the fact that not all humans have these capabilities, or the kinds that we might recognize.) What actually matters is that someone, not something, is being systematically slaughtered. They are murdered for meat.

Conditions inside factory farms and slaughterhouses look like scenes from a horror movie: "Layer hens" (who produce eggs) are crammed together in small cages where natural behaviors such as dust bathing and stretching their wings are totally frustrated. Pregnant pigs live in gestation crates so small they can't turn around. "Veal calves" are prevented from moving so their muscles stay soft. It's one of the most depressing twists of modern agriculture that we confine some of the most social animals (a characteristic that makes domestication possible) and deny them a chance to relate with each other, not to mention with us.

The slaughterhouse is a highly stressful environment. The killing lines move extremely fast. For instance, a single slaughterhouse may kill over 1,000 pigs per hour (Pig Transport and Slaughter, n.d.). Some animals are skinned alive or thrown into vats of boiling water while still conscious. Chickens are electrocuted in a water bath, which paralyses them for easier handling, but doesn't prevent pain. Layer hens and male chicks are sometimes ground alive in a garborator-like machine. Most food animals are murdered by throat-cutting ("sticking") and are kept alive while they bleed out. Food animals are also killed by "gassing, electrocution, beating to death, bulldozing live animals to pits" (Sorenson, 2010, p. 43).

Female animals in the food industry are raped and their reproductive systems are exploited: dairy cows are impregnated through a violent and invasive procedure and treated as milk machines, pigs are also impregnated, and chickens are forced to produce many more eggs than their bodies can handle. Male animals are also harmed. For example, bulls are forcibly ejaculated so cows can be artificially inseminated. These coercive physically forced forms of penetration are rape.

Animals' treatment within factory farms is antithesis to their natural ways of life. Whether scales, skin, fur, or feathers, underneath is someone of flesh and blood, with the capacity to feel pleasure and pain, and whose lives matter to them. But if these descriptions aren't enough to inspire some private doubts, try listening to the first agonizing minute of Propagandhi's track "Purina Hall of Fame" (from *Today's Empires, Tomorrow's Ashes*). According to Hannah, this song has moved people the most of any of their animal liberation songs. When we asked why, he replied, "Because it's real. It's not an abstraction. It's not an opinion. It is the facts-on-the-ground of animal exploitation shorn of the mythology and marketing of the industry" (Hannah, personal communication, August 1, 2012).

TOUCHING THE WEB

> And I'm still as stupid as anyone, but I know my mistakes. I have recognized one form of oppression, now I recognize the rest. (Hannah, 1996)

Speciesism is the "widely held belief that the human species is inherently superior to other species and so has rights or privileges that are denied to other sentient animals" (Ryder, n.d.). The ideology that humans are superior to other animals is speciesist, just as a belief that men are superior to women is sexist, and that white people are superior to People of Color is racist.

Learning about animal exploitation can be like tapping on a thread of a spider web: Touch one part, and the whole thing quivers. On the one hand, abuse of animals is rampant and more repugnant than fathomable, while on the other hand, this same exploitation in its dizzying scale and permutations is also inextricably attached to crappy ways we treat other people and the earth more generally. For example, slaughterhouses notoriously draw on marginalized workers whose bodies and minds are often brutalized in dangerous conditions. Capitalism considers these "unskilled workers" to be largely expendable. (Sound familiar?) The conditions in plants can contribute to stress that some take out on animals. At the same time, industrial animal agriculture pollutes the environment with gases such as methane, which promotes global warming and the poisoning of ground water. "When one really explores and tries to understand the underpinnings of an oppressive relationship, you start to see those underpinnings elsewhere, if not everywhere," reflects Hannah (personal communication, August 1, 2012).

DON'T DO NOTHING BECAUSE YOU CAN'T DO EVERYTHING

> And life's too short to make others' shorter—(animal liberation now!). (Hannah, 1996)

"Nailing Descartes to the Wall" ends with a call for "animal liberation now!" When asked what that means, Hannah replied, "First and foremost . . . it's a protracted war against the animals-as-food industry" (Hannah, personal communication, August 1, 2012). A diversity of tactics is needed in this fight. The majority of animal liberation activists engage in legal activities: boycotts, protests, rallies, education, animal law, or sanctuary work. But some activists have responded to the increasing terror and devastation inflicted on animals by intensifying their own efforts with direct action tactics. Whether opening cages to free languishing hens, ramming whale hunting boats, or burning down slaughterhouses, animal liberationists take direct action to have an immediate impact on animals' lives and cause financial damage to the profiteers of animal exploitation (Best & Nocella, 2004; Colling & Nocella, 2011).

Often forgotten is that animals are also fighting for lives (Hribal, 2009). Propagandhi sings about this resistance in "Potemkin City Limits" (from *Supporting Caste*), based on the true story about a pig named Francis who escaped from an Albertan slaughterhouse in 1990. He was on the run for several months until killed. A statue erected in his honor declares that Francis "earned his freedom." While his acts of resistance should be celebrated, it's hypocritical to believe that he has more of a right to life than other farm animals.

Francis' struggle for animal liberation now is undeniable. Some people believe that no harm is committed when animals are killed "humanely," and that the most they're owed is the minimization of pain as they die. Yet, animals also have a will to live. They value their lives, even if we don't. Jonathan Balcombe (2009), from the Physicians Committee for Responsible Medicine, argues that animals have interests in continuing their lives, which crucially includes seeking pleasure: They have a great capacity for joy and delight. Primates, for example, release pain-relieving endorphins when they groom each other, while rats enjoy being tickled and many animals engage in all sorts of non-reproductive sex. Evolutionary biologist Marc Bekoff (2007) proves that numerous animals empathize with each other (and sometimes even with those outside their social group and species!). Given their complex social and emotional capacities, it's clear that "life's too short to make others' shorter" (Hannah, 1996).

As we finish this chapter, food trucks scatter the park across the street, the hum of generators mixes with the rhythmic buzz of cicadas. The annual Rotary Rib Fest is here. Factory farms and slaughterhouses seem far away, detached from the swell of smiling people, their faces washed in sunlight, and takeout containers in hand. It seems obscene that any of those meals could have been Francis. The contrast between the park and what's happening to animals not far from here, and so many other places, can feel overwhelming. At the end of our conversation, Hannah shared a similar sentiment. He reflected,

> All this... is going on right now, non-stop, in my own city and I'm essentially powerless to stop it... I try not to think about that too much, because I find it humiliating. If I really did what I thought should be done, I would be in jail for the rest of my life. This paradox that can break our spirit if we dwell on it.... Maybe I'm trying to say "don't do nothing because you can't do everything"? (personal communication, August 1, 2012)

Our "small acts of love and rebellion" (to quote Painted Thin, another Winnipeg band!) do matter. They matter to Francis, and to anyone who needs help. Maybe giving a damn, and doing the best you can, whatever that means for you, is the most punk rock thing of all.

REFERENCES

Animal Voices Radio [Producer]. (2006, March 7). *Nailing Descartes to the wall: Propagandhi interview* [Audio podcast]. Retrieved from http://animalvoices.ca/2006/03/07/nailing-descartes-to-the-wall-propagandhi-interview

Balcombe, J. (2009). Animal pleasure and its moral significance. *Applied Animal Behaviour Science, 118*(3), 208–216.

Bekoff, M. (2007). *The emotional lives of animals: A leading scientist explores animal joy, sorrow, and empathy—and why they matter.* Novato, CA: New World Library.

Best, S. & Nocella II, A. J. (2004). *Terrorists or freedom fighters? Reflections on the liberation of animals.* New York, NY: Lantern Books.

Bryant, T., Chaudhuri, U., Jamieson, D., Moore, L. I., & Wolfson, D. (2006). Linking cultural and legal transitions. *Animal Law, 13*(29), 29–59.

Colling, S. & Nocella II, A. J. (2011). *Love and liberation: An animal liberation front story.* Williamstown, MA: Piraeus Books.

Hannah, C. (1996). Nailing Descartes to the wall [Recorded by Propagandhi]. On *Less talk, more rock* [CD]. San Francisco, CA: Fat Wreck Chords.

Hribal, J. (2009). *Fear of the animal planet: The hidden history of animal resistance.* Petrolia, CA: Counterpunch.

Kazez, J. (2010). *Animalkind: What we owe to animals.* Malden, MA: Wiley-Blackwell.

Monson, S. (Director). (2005). *Earthlings.* [Documentary]. United States: Nation Earth.

Noske, B. (1997). *Beyond boundaries: Humans and animals.* Montreal, Quebec: Black Rose Publishing.

Pig transport and slaughter. (n.d.). People for the Ethical Treatment of Animals. Retrieved from http://www.peta.org/issues/animals-used-for-food/pig-transport-slaughter.aspx

Rupke, N. (1990). *Vivisection in historical perspective.* London, UK: Routledge.

Ryder, R.D. (n.d.). *Speciesism.* Retrieved from http://www.62stockton.com/richard/speciesism.html

Sorenson, J. (2010). *About Canada: Animal rights.* Black Point, Nova Scotia: Fernwood Publishing.

PART III

RESISTANCE

CHAPTER 5

"FIGHT THE POWER" BY PUBLIC ENEMY

David Stovall

TO BANG, BLAST, AND STRUGGLE FOR FREEDOM

When I was first approached by the editors to contribute the following chapter, I was a bit conflicted. Public Enemy (PE) is one of my favorite groups of all time, but "Fight the Power" (Shocklee, Sadler, & Ridenhour, 1989) is not my favorite song (Black Steel in the Hour of Chaos is still the *ultimate* PE banger!). Despite the fact that it is considered one of their most, if not *the* most, important contributions (and one of the more important songs in Hip Hop, for that matter), I felt that it became the opus that unfortunately overshadowed the breadth and depth of their body of work. Nevertheless, despite its timelessness and current relevance, "Fight the Power" should be contextualized to the conditions and events of the late 1980s and the reality of how the song is a reflection of the lives of Black and Latino/a urban youth in that historical moment. Bridging the 1980s to the current moment, songs like "Fight the Power" have a critical connection that should be explored in relevance to the lives of the same group of young people. Wrongly interpreted by mainstream media as "rage-filled" or "hateful" music, the songs and lyrics of PE deserve to be understood as reflective of the counter-stories of oppressed peoples.

Rebel Music, pages 43–50

For the reasons listed above, the following chapter is a call to action more than a tribute. Because 22 years is a lifetime in the world of youth culture, PE and "Fight the Power" may appear ancient to some. However, as a college professor and volunteer high school social studies teacher, the song (and those like it) continually present a challenge to all adults who work with young people: *in our attempts to demonstrate solidarity with youth, we must be keenly aware and remain willing to engage the things we do not know.* Waxing poetic serves little purpose to young people who are dealing with the realities of high-stakes testing, homelessness, sexual exploitation, poverty, the prison industrial complex, the military industrial complex, racism, police brutality, gentrification, and disenfranchisement. We need to understand the current situation of young people in urban space as intense. For these reasons we must use this context to create thoughtful, clear, justice-oriented curriculum that work to develop the skills of our students to navigate and change the current reality—not as a lofty vision, but in the practical spaces that constitute the victories and defeats that we experience in the fight for educational justice.

Simultaneously, the following chapter is not a manifesto. Instead, it should be considered reflections on my own struggle to engage students with relevant, thoughtful, action-provoking curriculum in a moment when many of them have been deemed disposable by the State. Because many communities that have historically had the least are getting even less in terms of access to state, local, and federal resources, "Fight the Power" is both relevant and somewhat prophetic. In the rebellious and protest tradition of jazz, blues, folk, punk, and rock (i.e., Last Poets, Watts Prophets, Black Jazz Ensemble, Oscar Brown Jr., Abbey Lincoln, Max Roach, Odetta, Joan Baez, Bob Dylan, Woodie Guthrie, Pete Seger, The Clash, The Ramones, New York Dolls, etc.) "Fight the Power" provides social commentary accepted by few but understood by many.

Returning to the practical matters of the document, the chapter is divided into three sections. The first section engages the political, economic, and social context of the late 1980s for urban youth. Part two engages the song sonically and visually. Providing context for PE, the lyrics and visuals of "Fight the Power" provide an overlooked critique and call to action. As the visual advent of music video enhanced (or numbed) our connection to a particular song, "Fight the Power" is deeply connected to a particular socio-political revival. The concluding section connects the song to the present-day, placing it in the context of urban classrooms and the tangible connections to the current moment. Included is a discussion of how the neoliberal turn in education and society at large has intensified the struggle for justice. Highlighted in a set of examples of student, family, teacher and community resistance, the hope is for readers to understand the struggle and possibilities for equity and justice.

WELCOME TO THE TERRORDOME: THE WRATH OF THE 1980s, PROTEST AND THE POLITICS OF DISPOSABILITY

The decade predating the 1990 release of PE's album *Fear of a Black Planet* has particular significance in understanding the prominent underpinnings of a song like "Fight the Power." The devastation of the crack epidemic, along with government disinvestment in programming centered in social welfare (K–12 education, higher education, employment development programs, etc.) wreaked havoc on Black and Latino/a communities throughout the mid-1970s and 1980s. Continuing the legacy of de-industrialization in the 1970s, the subsequent War on Drugs heightened under the Reagan Administration utilized legislative tools like mandatory minimums and extended sentences (e.g., Rockefeller Laws in the state of New York) to imprison a generation of young African-American and Latino/a males. Excellently documented in the accounts of Alexander (2012), Wacquant (2009), and Brown (1999), the advent of the prison industrial complex (PIC) remains as one of the most totalizing forces that continues to deem a generation of young people as disposable. Due to its reciprocal effects through felony disenfranchisement (the process whereby convicted felons cannot vote or hold certain occupations depending on the laws of the state), underground economies are in some cases understood as the most viable means for sustenance.

Despite images of the flashy, opulent, over-indulgent drug-dealer/pimp archetype glamorized in 1970s Blaxploitation films like *Superfly or The Candy Tangerine Man,* this was not the case for the vast multitude of persons participating in the illicit drug-trade. Where many aspired to live the lives of Bumpy Johnson, Frank Lucas, and Nicky Barnes and their reincarnations in the form of Azie (AZ) Faison, Alberto (Alpo) Martinez, and Rich Porter in Harlem, "Freeway" Ricky Ross in Los Angeles, Flukey Stokes in Chicago, or the original 50-Cent in Queens, their opulence remained pipe dreams for most. Nevertheless an unusual relationship developed in many communities in urban America: for some, the drug kingpin became the anti-hero of sorts—despised by the larger world, they operated as the one group of people who were willing to support those who were down-and-out when few others would. Through their material support of the block, many understood the wrongdoings of the drug-dealer, but they were the few people who were willing to support the downtrodden. We knew their enterprise was problematic, but these men and women were often the people we grew up with who took "different paths" from the mainstream and began an engagement with a world with seismic risks for the prospect of considerable gains.

Conversely, there were also members of the same group of young people in urban spaces who began to educate themselves on the realities of racism not as solely a contemporary phenomenon, but as part of a larger historical continuum. College campuses across the country had thousands of students participating in campaigns against the Apartheid state in South Africa, nuclear proliferation, Israeli settlements, and police brutality at the local and national level. Popularized in the Artists Against Apartheid song "Sun City," numbers of mainstream artists were willing to lend their efforts to popularize the efforts of activists both locally and internationally.

In the later part of the decade, much of the divestment work loaned itself to a renaissance of the sentiment displayed in the Black Power movement of the late 1960s and early 1970s. Dubbed in many circles as Afro centricity or Afrocentrism, the international interest in the plight of People of Color internationally lent itself to return to a study of Black and Brown people in the United States. Books like Garter G. Woodson's *Miseducation of the Negro,* Harold Cruise's *The Crisis of the Negro Intellectual* and bell hooks' *Ain't I a Woman* were showing up in reading circles, challenging those who engaged to return to the idea that our communities were valuable and deserving of change. For a brief moment a burgeoning of African-American studies departments were beginning to expand to provide graduate degrees. K–12 educators began to re-incorporate ethnic studies into their social studies and history curricula. College students who transitioned the anti-Apartheid/divestment work onto local student and community struggles returned home to work for community organizations instead of Fortune 500 companies. National media coverage on the 1989 Virginia Beach Greekfest riots and the Tawana Brawley rape accusation had African-American students (and other students of color) question their position in the larger society. Police brutality, discrimination, and the perpetual regulation of Black bodies became rallying cries for scores of youth disillusioned with the ideal of the "American dream." Instead of looking outward for people to assist us in changing our conditions, the Afrocentric renaissance returned many to Ella Baker's notion that we are the ones we've been waiting for. For many, her sentiments held considerable weight in communities ravaged by policies of the Reagan administration coupled with local and state disinvestment.

Because the movement was not without its contradictions (our continued inability to critically engage sexism, homophobia, ageism, ableism, and anti-Semitism), it was one that resonated with young people in that it challenged common notions of an elite class that would provide the saving grace for the masses of poor, working class urban youth. In addition to PE, groups like X-Clan and their community partners the Blackwatch Movement were seemingly committed to the uplifting of historically disenfranchised communities. Paired with these sentiments, in many cities there was a sense of what was needed to reclaim our communities. The work of Sonny Carson in Brooklyn, New York was of particular importance as the video for "Fight the Power" was shot in conjunction with the Brooklyn March to End Violence.

For myself, this was my coming of age moment in that I was immersed in a space where people involved in the cultural, political, and nationalist movements were reaching back to the younger generation to pose alternatives for our current condition. As students at my high school became more versed with PE through albums like *Yo! Bum Rush the Show,* a growing militancy began to emerge in our consciousness. In addition to hearing songs like "Public Enemy #1" and "You're Gonna Get Yours," we also began to read the teachings of Malcolm X and H. Rap Brown. Earlier civil rights struggles became viewed as docile and accommodating. For a young person in the late 1980s, I was affirmed by the suggestion of taking power instead of asking for it.

As a Chicagoan, I was familiar with the Nation of Islam (NOI) and the teachings of Elijah Muhammad. By way of some relative independence granted by my parents (the ability to drive and take public transportation), I was able to venture out to other parts of the city. In the fall of 1988, one of my classmates (who was a member of the NOI) got a group of friends together in study hall and asked us to go to attend a service at Mosque Maryam (NOI national headquarters). Out of curiosity and my initial knowledge of PE, I thought it was definitely something to check out. The security detail of the NOI, commonly known as the Fruit of Islam (FOI) used to perform a precise military marching drill that was duplicated by members of PE known as the S1Ws (short for Security of the First World). Because some S1Ws were FOI members, the use of military drill was an exciting element to PE shows. All of my classmates were fascinated with this imagery and wanted to know more.

While I was truly impressed with the Minister Louis Farrakhan's oratory skills, I was equally astounded by the centrality of self-reliance and community development in his sermon. Some of my classmates were so impressed that two of them joined the NOI directly after the service. Despite the speech I remained a skeptic, as I wasn't as comfortable with their ideas around gender. Nevertheless, I respected Farrakhan's unwavering commitment to his beliefs. I wasn't used to hearing sentiment like his. The brash militancy and call to action was something that stuck with me. PE's songs were a way for me to localize many of the national struggles against racism and marginalization. As a young person I knew something was wrong in our communities, but I had no clue as how to address it. In this moment "Fight the Power" became the anthem by which to direct my energies.

INTO THE VISUAL: IMAGERY, REFLECTION AND "FIGHT THE POWER" AS FORMATIVE CONSCIOUSNESS RAISING

In the earlier years of music video production and television shows solely dedicated to the viewing of music videos, viewers were often treated to long-form or "full-length" videos. My preparation to write this chapter had me view the full-length version of "Fight the Power." In my own recollection, I hadn't watched the full-length video in at least 15 years. Totally forgotten was the footage from the 1963 March on Washington by Universal International Newsreel. The announcer states that the march was an attempt to end forever the blight of racial inequity. Directly following the footage the video transitions to a march in Brooklyn led by PE. Chuck D (lead emcee), is holding a megaphone and states:

> We rollin' this way—that march in 1963, that was a bit of nonsense. We ain't rolling like that no more—(as a) matter of fact, in young Black America we rollin' up with seminars, press conferences, and straight up rallies. Am I right? (crowd roars back—Yeah!) We gonna get what we got to get coming to us. Word up—we ain't going out like that '63 nonsense. (D'Ambrosio, 2005)

I had forgotten that the video had been positioned as a critique of the 1963 march through the use of similar imagery. Long placards that had the names of cities, states, and New York City boroughs were identical to the ones used in the March on Washington. What was different, however, was the addition of posters with seminal figures in African-American History (Harriet Tubman, Medgar Evers, Sojourner Truth, Malcolm X, Martin Luther King, Marcus Garvey, Angela Davis, etc.). Because our images of the March on Washington are passive in the sense of people holding hands and singing spirituals, imagery from the video for "Fight the Power" were visceral. Young people were orderly and at the same time excited, jumping up and down, holding up two fingers for peace, sitting on each other's shoulders and carrying banners that stretched across the street. The song was the rallying cry for the march, with young people yelling to "fight the power." The visuals were powerful in that they created another dimension for the song through the connection of song lyrics to celluloid imagery. For me, as a seventeen-year-old in 1989, the coupling was magical. Rarely did we see images of ourselves as young people claiming space and pushing to change our condition. Strengthening this concept was the fact that Spike Lee used "Fight the Power" as the unofficial theme song for his 1989 seminal film *Do the Right Thing*. The popularity of this film with my friends in high school made the video even more enticing.

Contributing to my personal excitement was the affirmation of my personal feelings about the music industry at large. Upon learning about the ingrained structural racism of the music business, Chuck D's verse was affirmation of the way I felt about Elvis as the "king" of rock and roll: "Elvis was a hero to most, But he never meant shit to me, Straight up racist that sucka was simple and plain, Motherfuck him and John Wayne!" (Shocklee, Sadler, & Ridenhour, 1989). The next few lines, "'Cause I'm Black and I'm proud, I'm ready and hyped plus I'm amped, Most of my heroes don't appear on no stamps" (Shocklee et al., 1989) were the ultimate voicing of truth to power at the time. Between N.W.A. and PE, the fact that someone was willing to tell the truth in an uncompromising way served as my inspiration to engage. It inspired me to learn more about Muddy Waters, Big Mama Thornton, Sister Rosetta Tharpe, Howlin Wolf, Dizzy Gillespie, Otis Dixon, Koko Taylor, Chuck Berry, Little Richard, and the countless R&B, jazz, blues, and soul artists that were never given their proper due. The veil of whiteness had been lifted to expose fallacy while encouraging others to right the wrongs of the current historical record. Hip Hop was at its punk moment when a bevy of artists began to name the unseen and overlooked.

WE ROCK ON AND ON AND ON AND ON: "FIGHT THE POWER" AS LEGACY AND PRAXIS

Instead of reminiscing about Hip Hop's "golden age," it's much more important to recognize the changing landscape of Hip Hop. The advent of corporate media influences along with the demise of the record company in its traditional sense has taken Hip Hop in an entirely different direction than its genesis in the South Bronx in the late seventies. The world of PE, Eric B. and Rakim, MC Lyte, Queen Latifah, Lakim Shabazz, Digable Planets, De La Soul, KRS-ONE, Gang Starr, EPMD, and X-Clan is not the world of 2 Chainz, Lil Wayne, LFMAO, Tyga, Nikki Minaj, Drake, Rick Ross, Meek Mill, and Wacka Flocka Flame. Where the end of the modern record company should provided more visibility to do-it-yourself artists, the corporate influence has morphed to use the same outlets to steer tastes and desire.

For these reasons and countless others, PE and "Fight the Power" deserve to be contextualized in the current milieu in the fight against disparities with regard to race, class, employment, housing, gender, sexuality, and ability. The same forces that Chuck D addressed in 1989 remain salient. Some of the faces may have changed, but the work remains the same. We are *still* the ones we've been waiting for.

REFERENCES

Alexander, M. (2012). *The new Jim Crow: Mass incarceration in the age of colorblindness.* New York, NY: New Press.

Brown, M. (1999). *Race, money and the American welfare state.* Ithaca, NY: Cornell University Press.

D'Ambrosio, A. (2005). Interview: Chuck D. *The Progressive.* Retrieved August 22, 2013, from www.progressive.org/mag_chuckd

Shocklee, H., Sadler, E., & Ridenhour, C. (1989). Fight the power [Recorded by Public Enemy]. On *Fight the power* [Cassette, single]. New York, NY: Motown Records.

Wacquant, L. (2009a). *Prisons of poverty.* Minneapolis, MN: University of Minnesota Press.

CHAPTER 6

"HERO OF WAR" BY RISE AGAINST

Scott Robertson

A funny thing happens to punk bands that have been around for a while; they get better. The years of practice, studio time, and touring begin to shape extremely talented musicians. Punk bands start writing songs that their parents actually begin to enjoy. Every so often, a heart-felt ballad finds its way onto an album and becomes an instant classic. Rise Against's acoustic ballad "Hero of War" (McIlrath, 2008) isn't simply a culmination of years or songwriting but a deep reflection of the pain suffered by soldiers in war. The song itself is a remarkable narrative of a soldier reflecting on his time in the second U.S.-led war on Iraq. Lead singer and writer Tim McIlrath not only gives us a song for his generation, but he also opens the door for critical reflection on war from the perspective of the soldier. However, the missing perspectives from the song also lead to a healthy debate on whose voices have value. McIlrath challenges the U.S. war hero narrative by breathing life into the reality of war and the effects it has on American soldiers. Although this song does not give voice to the innocent victims of war, it is, nonetheless, a piece of poetry that undercuts the heroic allusions of war that the military industrial complex has created. It exposes the lies that military recruiters tell youth. In this chapter I critically analyze "Hero of War," examining its strengths and weaknesses

Rebel Music, pages 51–58

while at the same time drawing on history and other perspectives. For instance, how are America's youth enchanted by the military? How can punk rock politically motivate and educate youth to see how power operates? How do youth recognize and resist mainstream narratives? These are just questions that scratch at the surface of "Hero of War." For the sake of space and clarity, this piece is not going to ask whether or not Rise Against has "sold out," nor will it be an in-depth response to war. Rather, it takes a critical look at just one of Rise Against's songs through one perspective of war, through one powerful genre.

"HERO OF WAR": ORIGINS

"Hero of War" appears on Rise Against's fifth studio album, *Appeal to Reason*. In an October 2008 interview with *The Red Alert* (McKibbin, 2008), Tim Mcllrath said that he approached his producer with an acoustic song written from the perspective of a war veteran. A serendipitous suggestion since the producer, Bill Stevenson (Descendents), had just been thinking that Rise Against needed an acoustic war protest song. So, the song made the album. This isn't Rise Against's only anti-war song ("Audience of One," "Survivor's Guilt") but one of their strongest since it was written as a reflection of war more than a critique of war or imperialism/empire, "I wanted to take the perspective of 'What is the war going to be looked back on as'" (McKibbin, 2008). Tim was already meeting returning vets out on the road, was reading the newspaper articles, and decided those voices deserved a channel to be heard. This was his way of "documenting what's going on, like other artists documented for their generation and for generations to come" (Sciarretto, 2008). Like many punk rockers, we come to learn about the world around us through music. So, in the tradition of so many Vietnam War era songs, Rise Against documents the horrors of war. Sensing that no other artists (perhaps he meant mainstream acts) were talking about the ill effects of (at the time) six years of occupation in Afghanistan and Iraq, Rise Against released "Hero of War."

HAVE YOU SEEN THE WORLD? ARMY STRONG

Flashback. I would be graduating in less than a year. "Class of 1997." I was always amazed how futuristic that year sounded. Senior year of high school was shaping up nicely, especially towards the back end when career days and college days would interrupt normal class time. "You mean I can leave campus and go check out Cerritos College and it's all OK?" "So we're not having economics, because some Army guy is going to come talk to us? I'll take the free pencil!" They didn't tell us that Sgt. Manzano would also be calling us every day, sounding like our best bud, trying to recruit us for the Army. It wasn't hard to see through the lies (Allison & Solnit, 2007). You can have your pencil back. How do I still remember the recruiter's name? Well, he made sure you knew his name because, see, it sounded like apple in Spanish, except with an "o" at the end. To this day, my old band mate and friend still recalls those late afternoon chats with Sgt. Manzano, who offered us a chance to "see the world." Fortunately for us, we had long been educated by the punk rock scene, devouring bands like Propagandhi, Bad Religion, F.Y.P., Millions of Dead Cops, and I-Spy. We also couldn't get enough of the pop-punk coming from the now iconic labels Fat Wreck Chords and Epitaph. We weren't swapping MP3s; we were trading CDs, vinyl, and cassettes of Lagwagon, Millencolin, Randy, Nofx, The Vandals, Guttermouth, The Descendents, No Use for a Name, Good Riddance, 88 Fingers Louie (now with members in Rise Against). Combined, these punk groups created a catalog of critical thought that we never received in high school. Propagandhi's first album *How to Clean Everything* taught us more than we ever learned in any high school history or social studies class. We saw how power operated in our society. Soon we attempted the vegan lifestyle, renounced patriarchy, sexism, homophobia, racism, capitalism, among many other "isms."

Haenfler (2012) points out what's at the core of punk: "Punk is about anti-conformity and countering hegemony" (p. 45), which allows punks to "reveal the inequalities of race/class/gender/sexuality and debate alternatives" (p.45). So, when Sgt. Manzano put on the heat to recruit us, we knew right away it would be a bad move. Bad Religion and Propagandhi introduced us to Noam Chomsky. After we read books from Chomsky to Zinn, Manzano had no chance of persuading us to join any army. We weren't going to become invaders protecting the wealth of the American elite. Yet, we recognized the privilege of our positions. Although we came from working class families, lived in an apartment complex situated in an auto-mall, we still received the benefits of white privilege. Our clothes may have been worn, but our teachers and counselors expected us to do well, and we did well enough. We were tracked into college preparatory classes. I avoided joining the military and went to a state college, my friend worked at an ice-hockey shop, not starting community college for a good four years after graduation, yet he eventually finished law school. Had we grown up just a decade or so later, listening to manufactured radio rock, we might not be in the places we are today.

We didn't just have to battle military recruiters. Yeah, we saw *Top Gun* over and over again. We grew up with *GI-Joe*. We were also inundated with a seemingly pro-war news media in the early 1990s. Guns were cool, sure, but that was it, just cool. Today, the same cartoons, movies, and news media exist, perhaps to a more violent degree. But kids today are also not simply surrounded by pro-war imagery; they are taken into it virtually. Games like *Call of Duty* and the Army's official video game, *America's Army* (americasarmy.ca), don't simply make guns cool, but so badass that kids want to fire them. The Army is now directly engaged in controlling the beliefs and attitudes of children. Even if you don't play video games, you may get recruited at a punk concert or a sporting event. "How many pull-ups can you do?" "*Son, have you seen the world?*" (McIlrath, 2008). The Marines even directly market to punk rock youth with their slogan, "Marines move towards the sounds of chaos." The Navy also uses propaganda to recruit. They ask if your life is worth writing about. Why should you have a desk job when you can explore the open seas? A Navy recruiting center near my home has "Heroes Don't Brag" stenciled on the large front windows. Why not become an elite soldier? "The few, the proud, the Marines." "*What would you say if I said that you could?*" (McIlrath, 2008). And this battle of marketing isn't only waged on kids. If you watch enough TV you may have seen Army commercials targeted at parents, encouraging parents to be supportive of their child's wishes to join the Army. Watch your daughter blossom into a soldier. In fact, I would say underlining these commercials is the idea that in order to be a good parent, you will let your child join the Army. Don't you want your son or daughter to be a *hero of war*?

A SOLDIER'S VOICE: LOOKING BACK

You were going to get money for college, see the world, and hopefully blow some buildings up. Now you are back home after years of extended duty, and you don't want to live any more. For the first half of 2012, nearly one veteran soldier committed suicide per day (Burns, 2012). Your Sergeant Manzano didn't tell you about post traumatic stress disorder (PTSD), and I doubt you heard much about the depleted uranium that you would handle. Staff Sergeant Robert Bales did how many tours, killed how many innocent Afghan women and children? How can anyone understand the things you've seen and done? Civilians will never get how lucky they are to be able to walk past a public trashcan without the fear of an IED going off inside. In fact, most people won't understand, and this alienation has long been a part of what it means to be a war veteran.

Rise Against approaches you and lets you know that yes, we will never know the pain you've endured, but let us try to share with others your story. They show just how easy it was to join. You get to carry a gun, and you even get paid. That sounds pretty good. You joined the group, cut your hair short, and learned to march in sync. You chanted hymns such as "Blood makes the grass grow." Your muscles began to swell; you really were becoming Army Strong. You could already see the hero's welcome, a home-town parade just for you! "*They'll be so damn proud of me*" (McIlrath, 2008). You had fought for your family and country. You are a true hero of war.

"*I kicked in the door, I yelled my commands*" (McIlrath, 2008). This didn't happen in Call of Duty. You don't recall the screaming babies, the wife pleading that you not take her husband. It was hard, but you had to protect America from terror. You humiliated a father, a husband, took part in your own version of terror, not once, but "*again and again.*" Of course you felt like shit after, but you felt better at the thought of returning home as a hero of war. As you listen to Rise Against, you know this song isn't against you; it's just your story. You never said it was innocent. Returning to patriotism helps sooth the soul, "*I'll carry this flag to the grave if I must*" (McIlrath, 2008). Sadly though, night raids aren't the worst part of the war experience. And when you come home, you'll learn that you weren't gathering useful information as you were lead to believe. You may even start to see your actions as acts of terror.

You killed an innocent. You "*asked her to stop.*" You "*begged her to stay, but she pressed on.*" You lifted your gun and "*fired away*" (McIlrath, 2008). Numb. How can a punk rock singer understand? How can some punk academic understand this? Can you tell your mother? No way is this a bed time story for your daughter. This is your memory, your torment, your flashback.

You get your hero's welcome, some medals and scars. You can see that they're proud but they do not know. You have seen the world.

COMING HOME

> I was willing to die for this country. I trusted this government. Now over 6,000 of my brothers and sisters in uniform are dead in a war we know the politicians lied about. Over 1 million Iraqis and Afghans are dead for some billionaires' access to resources and defense contracts. I stopped participating in their wars for their profits. It's our right to refuse to sacrifice our lives and the lives of others for Wall Street's profits. (Prysner, 2012)

On May 21, 2012 outside the NATO Summit in Chicago, Tim McIlrath performed "Hero of War" in front of thousands of protestors. Afghan and Iraq War veterans came to "return" their medals. Over fifty veterans spoke on a make-shift stage, sharing their experiences of war with the demonstrators. After each concluded their speech, they threw their Global War on Terrorism medals into the direction of the NATO summit, landing on the street below. Not all veterans feel this way, and the responses to "Hero of War" also vary. In an interview with *Artist Direct*, McIlrath said that he would receive e-mails from vets thanking him for the song while other vets condemned it (Sciarretto, 2008).

What we have here is a debate, absent in the corporate media. To find it, one has to be engaged in the subculture or already turned on to alternate media sources like Democracy Now! This is what punk politics is all about: raising issues that your high school civics teacher or your local evening news anchor have no idea exist. Punk is really exploring how power works culturally, economically, socially, and politically. What hierarchies exist, and what inequalities are built into the structure and fabric of our society? How do we change the prevailing order?

THE VOICES OF THE OTHER

Rise Against does a wonderful job of sharing the voice of an American soldier, victimized by his own country, in a war whose motives he can't defend. Can we say that this song is anti-war? It can't be too hard to imagine that many people would say that the difficulties our "hero" faced were merely consequences of war. Yes, war is ugly, but we need war to protect our freedoms. Perhaps this is exactly what you've been saying this whole time. You might even say that this song is just another corporate anti-war song; one that sounds political, but has no pull to incite any real action. Malott and Peña (2004) considered the Dead Kennedy's "Holiday in Cambodia" a "limited criticism of war" (p. 103). Perhaps the same could be said here. For a punk band, it isn't exactly risky to be anti-war. In fact, what kinds of punk bands aren't anti-war?

As September 11, 2001 slipped from recent memory and the War on Terrorism was in full swing, music acts felt safe again to "speak out." Bands were eager to get onto Fat Wreck Chords compilation, *Rock Against Bush.* MTV-friendly punk bands like Yellowcard, who cater to young teens with their melodic pop punk, were also branding themselves as anti-war. Green Day made it fashionable and safe to be "critical" of the U.S. government. Is Rise Against's "Hero of War" just another "anti-war" song that record labels feel safe to publish? However, it wasn't easy for all bands. Propagandhi had their song "Bullshit Politicians" removed from the *Rock Against Bush* compilation because of a liner note poking fun at George Soros, a big financier behind MoveOn.Org. In the punk world, if a song was safe to print by a major record label, then surely it didn't ruffle enough feathers. Rise Against shouldn't have to write an all-encompassing anti-war manifesto, and I wouldn't expect them to, but what they leave out of the song is truly worth discussing. I encourage the reader to find anti-war songs, search YouTube, even check Wikipedia; what I believe you will find are lists and lists of anti-war songs that come from the personal perspective of the invader, the soldier, the protestor, or the armchair activist. These songs critique the motives and costs of the war. Although they justly criticize warmongers, they often fail to see the perspective of those on the receiving end of the bombs. Even the most critical Vietnam War films center on the U.S. soldier experience. It's interesting to note that the official music video for "Hero of War" mirrors this film style.

When are we going to hear the song written from the Iraqi child's perspective? From the child frozen in a state of shock after seeing her parents literally blown away? From the boy whose father was murdered by American troops hovering above in an Apache helicopter firing down bullets into their family van as the father attempts to help injured civilians? So often, even in the anti-war movement, our due attention is not paid to those that suffer most. Perhaps we should hear about the victims of war before we are ready to spin the "heroes" of war into the victims. Rise Against tells the hero's story, but as sad as it may be, the situation is far worse on the other side. Until we recognize how we're connected to the true victims of war, only then can we explore how we have become victims ourselves. Only when we can put faces to collateral damage will we finally be able to put faces on ourselves.

RISE AGAINST

Fortunately for us, punk rock can respond. Although uncommon, we can hear the perspectives of the oppressed. Underground punk bands don't have the same filters that mainstream acts have. You will hear the voices not found on television. This is one of punk rock's greatest strengths. It opens up political dialog wider than the mainstream corporate conversation. Propagandhi wrote "Mate Ka Moris Ukum Rasik An" about Bella Gahlos, a defect from East Timor, whose family was murdered under General Suharto's rule. Rise Against also gives us "Prayer of the Refugee." Punk rock is capable of exploring all the angles. Punk bands respond to neo-Nazi bands, hardcore Christian bands, mainstream bands, straight-edge bands, and so on. O'Hara (1999) offers a nice history of competing subgenres and shows how movements can check each other. Bands with the same progressive positions can counter each other through song about strategy and activism. Punk rock bands create an underground network of ideas that can go infinitely to the left or right. When you go to school or watch television news you receive a narrow world view. It is no wonder then that many people, like myself, have completely re-written their lives after listening to a punk song.

REFERENCES

Allison, A. & Solnit, D. (2007). *Army of none: Strategies to counter military recruitment, end war, and build a better world.* New York, NY: Seven Stories Press.

Burns, R. (2012, June 7). Military suicide rate surges to nearly one per day this year. *The Huffington Post.* Retrieved August 21, 2013 from http://www.huffingtonpost.com/2012/06/07/military-suicide-surges-_n_1578821.html

Haenfler, R. (2012). Punk ethics in the mega-university. In Z. Furness (Ed.), *Punkademics: The basement show in the ivory tower* (pp. 37–48). Brooklyn, NY: Minor Compositions.

Malott, C. & Peña, M. (2004). *Punk rockers' revolution: A pedagogy of race, class, and gender.* New York, NY: Peter Lang Publishing.

McIlrath, T. (2008). Hero of war [Recorded by Rise Against]. On *Appeal to reason* [CD]. Santa Monica, CA: Interscope.

McKibbin, A. (2008, October). Rise Against: A conversation with Tim McIlrath. *The red alert.* Retrieved August 23, 2013 from http://www.theredalert.com/features/riseagainst2.php

O'Hara, C. (1999). *The philosophy of punk: More than noise*! Oakland, CA: AK Press.

Prysner, M. (2012, July 12). Troops who say "No!" *OurLivesOurRights.Org.* Retrieved August 19, 2013 from http://www.ourlivesourrights.org/photo-viewer.html?photo_url=http://www.ourlivesourrights.org/photo-submissions/mike.jpg#.VCNFVLHQqn4

Sciarretto, A. (2008, December 14). Interview: Rise Against. *Artist direct.* Retrieved August 22, 2013 from http://www.artistdirect.com/nad/news/article/0,,4894898,00.html

PART IV

REBELLION

CHAPTER 7

"HIP HOP IS DEAD" BY NAS

Michael Benitez Jr.

INTRODUCTION

Many artists, critics, scholars, and fans alike have, throughout the past decade, engaged in a prolonged dialogue over the state of Hip Hop and the extent to which Hip Hop is either dead or dying. Ever since the bricks and rods were laid out and the foundation paved, Hip Hop has become a worldwide phenomenon that serves as a vehicle of agency through which many oppressed people's voices are heard and their stories told. Conversely, Hip Hop in its cultural expressive form has also become a genre of preference for many who do not directly identify with the experiences and struggles faced by the very same youth who pioneered the movement. In the late 1980s and into the 1990s, Hip Hop was soon met with corporate intrusion and money vultures seeking profit by commoditizing Hip Hop culture and capitalizing on its gained popularity, eventually leading to what is now a constant debate putting to question the extent to which Hip Hop remains credible and whether or not what is being produced is Hip Hop or, as Dyson (2004) alludes to, pop rap. I like to refer to this fusion of pop and rap as *pap*.

While many Hip Hop artists have come and gone, some have been able to adapt and transcend time, switching up their game over the years in

Rebel Music, pages 61–69

order to remain relevant while staying true to the social issues that continue to plague inner cities and urban communities. One of these Hip Hop artists is Queens-bred Nasir Jones, mainly known and recognized in the rap game as Nasty Nas or Nas. Nas's debut album *Illmatic* was released in 1994 and quickly became an instant classic with hits like *The Genesis, N. Y. State of Mind, One Love,* among others. Since then, Nas has released a flurry of mix tapes and albums, including *Hip Hop is Dead* in 2006. While all the other albums Nas dropped did not quite enjoy the same classic status as his *Illmatic,* Nas has always been able to stay on top of his game in order to remain fresh, relevant, and a top emcee in the Hip Hop music industry. No doubt he will go down as one of the nicest—if not *the* nicest—of his time, with fresh beats by the illest producers, dope rhymes, and sick punch-lines. His last two albums have also stirred up quite the controversy with *Hip Hop is Dead* and thereafter in 2008, *Untitled*—which he originally was going to title *Nigger,* triggering a stir of sentiments and responses about the use of the racially charged term (Nas drops "Nigger" album title, 2008). Hence, bringing me to my intention with this chapter.

So what exactly is the difference between Hip Hop yesterday and Hip Hop today? Is there a difference? Who gets to define what does or does not constitute Hip Hop? Is it the people, the clothes, the dialect, the aesthetic? Is it urban America, an industry, a culture? Is it a way of being, acting, thinking, living? And why is it critical for today's educators to afford Hip Hop the same respect afforded to other generations defined by their historical and sociopolitical context and conditions? In this chapter I aim to answer these questions using Nas's song as an important discourse in the use of Hip Hop as social movement. Thus, I provide a cultural lens into, and analysis of, Nas's song, *Hip Hop is Dead* (Jones, 2006a) from his 2006 album in the space of Hip Hop. In doing so, I provide a brief understanding of Hip Hop culture and the sociopolitical context it is situated in, further elucidate the message of Nas's message from a cultural perspective, and end by speaking to the value inherent in Hip Hop as a tool for transforming consciousness in education.

THE CULTURE THAT MADE NAS

I got so many rhymes I don't think I'm too sane
Life is parallel to Hell but I must maintain
And be prosperous, though we live dangerous
Cops could just arrest me, blamin us, we're held like hostages
It's only right that I was born to use mics
And the stuff that I write, is even tougher than dykes. (Jones, 1994)

The quote above from Nas's first album, *Illmatic*, provides a bit of insight into the lived experiences of Black urban youth and many Hip Hop artists' preference to relay their story and message utilizing poetic artistry in the form of rap music, while also doing it a manner that is aesthetically playful and, simultaneously, raw. Close to half a decade has passed since the marking of what many today refer to and have come to know as Hip Hop— a cultural movement, enduring phenomenon, and adaptive form of self-being and expression that presently speaks to the psyche of many but is rooted in the historic struggle of oppressed people forgotten by a system that ignored conditions of racism and hardships of urban poverty. One can trace Hip Hop culture, primarily recognized as rap, to ancient African oral traditions that have influenced contemporary African American cultural practice (Dyson, 2004), including the radical genius and entrepreneurial prowess of legends such as the late Gil Scott-Heron, Last Poets, DJ Kool Herc, African Bambatta, and Mele Mel, among others, from the gritty streets of New York City. It won't be long before the likes of Nas, Jay-Z, and 2-Pac also become legends, though they are already legends in the context of respective cohort generation. Such legends are what can be described as Hip Hop geniuses. Sam Seidel (2011) describes Hip Hop genius as the creative resourcefulness in the face of limited resources or flipping something out of nothing. Thus, Hip Hop does not reflect an inability of inner city youth who do not make it in mainstream or popular culture. Rather, Hip Hop is a representation of subjects and voices stemming from Black youth culture that has since the conception of slavery been discriminated against, marginalized, and/or denied equitable opportunities at attaining mobility in a society. Hip Hop critiques a society that unfortunately continues to devalue Black culture and/or non-white culture. Rooted in the 1970s and early 1980s as a form of resistance to oppressive conditions and as an alternative to mainstream media that did not reflect the experiences of inner city communities, Hip Hop has over the past four decades shaped and informed the values and ideas of many who have grown up listening and relating to Hip Hop, grown with it, and helped shape it. This includes many of today's Hip Hop artists as well as middle-aged professionals from urban communities across different economic and political sectors of society (i.e., health, law, education, government). However, it is important to note that Hip Hop as a culture may have influenced many, but it will always remain at the helm of youth cultural expression. This is critical to understand as Hip Hop relies on the youth to continuously redefine and refresh what Hip Hop looks like based on the needs and issues faced of the time and context. Thus, it is a culture primarily cultivated by youth who continue to face societal, economic, and political challenges and hardships pressed onto those who reside in inner cities of the United States, and eventually expanded to include struggles beyond inner cities and outside U.S. borders.

THE ELEMENT OF RAP (MCEEING)

Though Hip Hop's elements transcend the musical modules of the movement beyond "Mceeing" and "DJing" to include Graffiti (Hip Hop in form of artistry and breakdancing, Hip Hop in the form of dance), it is through its musical elements, largely, that most people experiencing similar conditions of poverty, hardship, and strife across the globe have been introduced to it and the sociopolitical realities that inform it. It is also from this elemental tradition of rap in Hip Hop that this chapter will be addressed. Rap is a form of lyrical and oratory flow that Trica Rose (1994) describes as "a black cultural expression that prioritizes lack voices from the margins of Urban America" (p. 2). Hence, Hip Hop culture provides a space where Black youth (African-American, Afro- Caribbean) primarily, and to some extent other racially minoritized groups from New York City, could be creative, innovative, and are encouraged to engage their entrepreneurial spirits in order to rise above the pit of poverty and racism as described by Mumia Abu-Jamal:

> ...the music arises from a generation that feels with some justice that they have been betrayed by those who came before them. That they are at best tolerated in schools, feared on the streets, and almost inevitably destined for the hell-holes of prison. They grew up hungry, hated and unloved. And this is the psychic fuel that generates the anger that seems endemic in much of the music and poetry. One senses very little hope above the personal goals of wealth to climb above the pit of poverty. (Immortal Technique, 2003)

Hip Hop culture has become a vanguard of social commentary that aesthetically aims to challenge the conditions in which Hip Hop culture has fermented. The flipside is that while much rap has positive and uplifting conscious messages, there is also much rap that reinforces practices of internalized oppression and display Black and non-white youth cultures in a negative light. This includes, but is not limited to, romanticized ghettoism (i.e., drugs, poverty, etc.), misogynistic representations and disrespect of women, overemphasis on materialism, and reinforcement of violence within these very same communities. And though much of this cultural insight into Hip Hop culture is very real, there are those rappers who shed light on these issues differently. Tricia Rose (1994) goes on to describe this paradox:

> Rap music brings together a tangle of some of the most complex social, cultural, and political issues in contemporary American society. Rap's contradictory articulations are not signs of absent intellectual clarity; they are a common feature of community and popular cultural dialogues that always offer more than one cultural, social, or political viewpoint. (p. 2)

On one hand you have rappers who make an effort to raise awareness about the lived experiences of young Black and Brown youth—sort of like a verbal museum of how the broader system impacts their lives. On the other hand, you have rappers who rap about these same issues in a commoditized manner, where dominant and monetary value is assigned to oppressive representations of minoritized people. Unfortunately, this latter approach benefits the profit-driven mission of media corporations at the expense of Hip Hop culture and humanity. Hence, the Hip Hop aesthetics (a way of expression without rules and boundaries that encourages liberation creativity, learning, speaking without fear, peer reinforcement, and a need to be heard) often utilized to pass on the message that guides much of Hip Hop lyricism has been partly high jacked by corporate entertainment giants. It is here at this production of knowledge threshold between authentic and commoditized representations of Hip Hop culture that Nas's song "Hip Hop is Dead" is situated.

NAS's HIP HOP IS DEAD

In the 2006 release of his studio album *Hip Hop is Dead,* Nas titled one of his tracks after the album. His album is a challenge to the Hip Hop world about the state of Hip Hop; in particular, the rap game. In his song "Hip Hop is Dead," featuring will.i.am of the Black Eyed Peas, Nas takes on the topic head on, which lead to others shining in and responding to Nas's cultural and political message on the state of Hip Hop. In the chorus itself he goes on to rap, "if Hip Hop should die before I wake/ I'll put and extended clip and body 'em all day/ roll to every station wreck the DJ/ roll to every station, wreck the DJ" (Jones, 2006a). Culturally speaking, Nas engages in a satiric and raw conversation with his listeners, proposing to go after the disc jockeys (DJs) who no longer have the independence to play to the taste and call of its cultural base. Instead, DJs are under an obligation to play a repeated play list of co-opted "pap" provided by the corporations who own the air waves as a result of the Telecom Act of 1996 that deregulated ownership restrictions on media outlets. This led to fewer companies owning the radio stations and having control over public consumption of music. The result: pop rap with very little social commentary, if any; pop rap often focuses on making dollars, spreading misogynistic messages, materialism, and individual mobility (not to be confused for individual style—very much a symbol of Hip Hop) without the collective community that makes Hip Hop what it is. I recall prior to 1996 being able to listen to Hip Hop vibes from different cultural locations that represented local tastes and diverse forms of Hip Hop. Today, it doesn't matter where you go because chances are radio stations are playing the same shortened playlists. Thus, his challenge that Hip Hop is dying may be partly directed to the DJs, but behind the lyrics he targets the corporations who make the decisions and the artists who buy into businesses' demoralized money making philosophy. Even at the beginning of the video production for the song, the screen reads:

> A new law has been passed today by the U.S. government. Hip Hop has been abolished and is no longer to be heard. All claiming the title MC will be arrested and given the worst penalty under the law. (Terrero, 2006)

In the track, he also goes on to rap, "everybody sound the same/commercialize the game/reminiscing' when it wasn't all business/it forgot where it started/so we all gather here for the dearly departed" (Jones, 2006a). His message has more to do more with a corporeal intrusion and commercialization, free speech infringement, and a departure from the roots of Hip Hop, as opposed to the death of Hip Hop. He illustrates this in the following lyrics: "Went from turntables to MP3s/ From 'Beat Street' to commercials on Mickey D's/ From gold cables to Jacobs/ From plain facials to Botox and face lifts" (Jones, 2006a).

In the track "Hip Hop is Dead," Nas also hints at other underlying issues that often go unnoticed without a critical ear to the lyrical verbiage he spits, such as knowledge representation and neocolonial dependence. The issue of knowledge representation deals with the production of knowledge through Hip Hop and should bring to light questions such as: Who is producing the music being consumed and under what conditions? Who is making decisions about the content of the music? Whose message is it? What Hip Hop music exists that is not receiving any air time and why? Who is listening to, and consuming public controlled radio? These questions are all important to consider given the deep history of corporate culture and social movements (i.e., abolition of slavery, civil rights movements; musical genres such as jazz, blues, and funk, etc.). One of his better tracks that gets at these issues of knowledge representation, I believe, is his collaboration with Damian Marley on their collaborative album *Distant Relatives* (Jones & Marley, 2010). In it they rhyme: "Discovering the world before this world. A World buried in time/uncover with rhymes. It gets no realer." Both Nas and Damian Marley provide provocative, insightful, and critical verses about knowledge in their song "Patience." First Damian Marley shines in with:

> On the TV the picture is/Savages in villages/And the scientist still can't explain the pyramids, huh/Evangelists making a living on the videos of ribs of the little kids/Stereotyping the image of the images And this is what the image is. (Nas & Marley, 2010)

Nas chimes in with challenging epistemological questions, "Who made up words? who made up numbers? And what kind of spell is mankind under?" He goes on to question our consciousness of neocolonialism when he rhymes:

> Anything along the land we consuming/Eatin', deletin', ruin/Trying to get paper/ Gotta have land, gotta have acres/So I can sit back like Jack Nicholson/Watch niggas play the game like the Lakers. (Nas & Marley, 2010)

Both Nas's and Damian's indictment of knowledge representation is quite evident in the lyrics; however, neocolonialism is another issue exposed indirectly, yet rather swiftly. Therefore, it is important to also illuminate the role of neocolonialism on Hip Hop culture, which refers to the dependence by the people on the structure to live and survive, thus having to adhere to some extent to the cultural practices of the dominant and ruling group.

In the track, "Hip Hop is Dead," Nas goes on to rap, "Any ghetto will tell ya', Nas helped grow us up/ my face once graced promotional Sony trucks/ hundred million and billin', I helped blow 'em up" (Jones, 2006a). His lyrics towards the end of his first verse suggest a dependence on each other by both the artist (the people) and the structure (the corporation). Nas's sales produced massive profit for the record companies he partnered with. In turn, Nas also implicates himself by admitting to: 1) helping the entertainment corporations get bigger and 2) benefiting financially from his partnership with the record label. As such, it is important to also illuminate how Nas himself has engaged in the poetic process that on one hand tells an important story, and on the other hand has worked to perpetuate the very same stereotypes about women, violence, and materialism through his lyrical candidness. Still, Nas makes it a point to remind us that he hasn't bought into the glamour of creating Hip Hop with no substance at the expense of the values and ethics that inform Hip Hop, as illustrated in the lyrics of "Let there be Light" (also on the album *Hip Hop is Dead*):

> No gang banging in New York tonight
> Just murals of Biggie Smalls, bigger than life
> Turn up the kid mic cuz ya'll ain't listening right
> What's all this talk that Nas got bought?
> I'd rather outline my body in white chalk. (Jones, 2006c)

Conversely, Nas uses his lyrics to continuously also remind us about the harsh cultural lived experiences and realities behind Hip Hop and the dangers associated with consuming ghettoized ideologies without addressing the conditions that have over time made Hip Hop a powerful and attractive avenue for urban youth identity development (Dyson & Daulatzai, 2010).

Other tracks on the album *Hip Hop is Dead* reiterate the influences of Hip Hop culture, such as in the lyrics of "Black Republican":

> Could it be the forces of darkness
> Against hood angels of good that forms street politics
> Makes a sweet honest kid turn illegal for commerce
> To get his feet out of them Converse (Jones, 2006b)

As Nas explained in an interview with MTV:

> When I say "hip-hop is dead," basically America is dead. There is no political voice. Music is dead... Our way of thinking is dead, our commerce is dead.... what I mean by "hip-hop is dead" is we're at a vulnerable state. If we don't change, we gonna disappear like Rome. Hip-hop is Rome for the 'hood. I think hip-hop could help rebuild America, once hip-hoppers own hip-hop.... We are our own politicians, our own government, we have something to say. We're warriors. (Reid, 2006)

Thus Nas's lyrics, as well as much of Hip Hop lyricism in general, could be a powerful tool no different than the books already utilized for teaching about social ills that continue to plague the lives of youth and the youth movements that continue to challenge the conditions created by those in positions of power and privilege. This includes educators associated with, and implicated in, education. In many ways, Hip Hop culture has recently, more than before, managed to permeate and exert its way into the soul of academia and helped cultivate a collective of students and educators alike to conceptualize Hip Hop as a means for teaching, learning, and raising consciousness. Given the rise in interest and use of Hip Hop in education and the academy, it is important to consider how Hip Hop can be effectively utilized as an educational pedagogy both in form and in content to examine the use of Hip Hop as a way to learn about cultural spaces. Hip Hop as pedagogy offers direct insight into lived experiences and realities of minoritized racial and ethnic people who have faced and continue to encounter oppression and marginalization. Nas's critical insight and controversial position on Hip Hop illuminates a need to reclaim the role of Hip Hop for generations to come. If more than anything, what his "Hip Hop is Dead" track suggests is that Hip Hop culture will always be around as long as there are: 1) social ills such as poverty and racism plaguing different communities and 2) new generations springing up that will use Hip Hop to tell their story their way. Ultimately, as long as there is a youth base faced with these issues, there will always be Hip Hop.

REFERENCES

Dyson, M. E. (2004). The culture of hip hop. In M. Forman & M. A. Neal, *That's the joint: The hip hop studies reader* (pp. 61–68). New York, NY: Routledge.

Dyson, M. E., & Daulatzai, S. (Eds.). (2010). *Born to use mics: Reading Nas's Illmatic.* New York, NY: Basic Civitas Books.

Immortal Technique. (2003). Homeland security and hip hop [featuring Mumia Abu-Jamal]. On *Revolutionary volume 2* [CD]. New York, NY: Viper Records.

Jones, N. (1994). New York state of mind [Recorded by Nas]. On *Illmatic* [CD]. New York, NY: Columbia.

Jones, N. (2006a). Hip hop is dead [Recorded by Nas]. On *Hip Hop is Dead* [CD]. New York, NY: Def Jam.

Jones, N. (2006b). Black Republican [Recorded by Nas]. On *Hip Hop is Dead* [CD]. New York, NY: Def Jam.

Jones, N. (2006c). Let there be light [Recorded by Nas]. On *Hip Hop is Dead* [CD]. New York, NY: Def Jam.

Jones, N., & Marley, D. (2010). Patience [Recorded by Nas]. On *Distant Relatives* [CD]. Los Angeles, CA: Universal Republic and Def Jam.

Nas drops "Nigger" album title: Controversial release will now be untitled. (2008, May 20). *First for Music News.* Retrieved August 22, 2013 from http://www.nme.com/news/nas/36731

Reid, S. (2006, October 10). MTV News Exclusive: Nas Previews *Hip-Hop Is Dead*... the N. *MTV News.* Retrieved on August 28, 2013 from http://www.mtv.com/news/articles/1542740/mtv-news-exclusive-nas-previews-new-lp.jhtml

Rose, T. (1994). *Black noise: Rap music and black culture in contemporary America.* Hanover, NH. Wesleyan University Press.

Seidel, S. (2011). *Hip hop genius: Remixing high school education.* New York, NY: Rowman and Littlefield.

Terrero, U. (Director). (2006). Hip hop is dead [Music video]. New York, NY: Def Jam.

CHAPTER 8

"PICTURES OF WOMEN GIVING BIRTH SELL RECORDS" BY OI POLLOI

Comrade Black

Do-it-yourself (DIY) punk saved my life... Literally. I owe everything about who I have become and all I have accomplished to DIY punk culture. If I had never known that a better world could be possible, if only I decided to do the work to create change, I would have been swallowed by the self destructive culture I grew up in. DIY punk is based on the idea of building community centered on certain values. Central to the punk ethos is a particular conception of DIY: an ethic that says you do not need to accept what you have been given or wait for anyone else to fix your problems for you. DIY ethic emerged out of punk culture and argues that we need not depend on those in power to solve personal, community, or even global problems. We can do things for ourselves, whether as individuals, or as a community.

> Perhaps the only canon of punk, true across all musical styles and subcultures, is that if you want to do something you should just go out and do it yourself. Don't wait for permission or approval, start a band, book a show, design a flier,

Rebel Music, pages 71–77

> publish a zine, plan a tour. If there's something that needs to be done, do it. (Potter, 2011, p. 102)

This ethos is based in the belief that if we take responsibility for ourselves and our own community, we don't need corporations, governments, or anyone to make our decisions for us. "There is no authority but yourself" (Crass, 1983). DIY punk is most noted for being in opposition to capitalism, corporations, mass production, and over-consumption.

AR CÀNAN, AR CEÒL, AR-A-MACH—OUR MUSIC, OUR LANGUAGE, OUR REVOLUTION

There is a strange story the mainstream music press likes to tell of punk. Generally it starts with the Sex Pistols or the Ramones, or other well known bands like The Clash. "The pundits who claim that punk grew out of bands like The New York Dolls, and then found its expression in The Sex Pistols, have totally missed the point: The Pistols were incidental, it could have been anyone" (Rimbaud, 1998, p. 79). These bands all had big hits on the radio and made it to the top of the pop charts. The story continues with other well known bands like The Velvet Underground, and somehow they always seem to end with the Seattle grunge rock band Nirvana. What makes this story so strange is that while all of these bands are well known on the radio and MTV, few, if any, would be found in the record collections of most kids sporting green Mohawks or dread mullets and septum piercings today. Absent from this list are the names of bands that can be found on nearly every punk kid's patch pants and jackets, legendary underground bands such as: Crass, Aus-Rotten, Conflict, DOOM, MDC, Amebix, Minor Threat, Nausea, Discharge, or Oi Polloi.

Oi Polloi formed in 1981, a year after I was born. They were touring and had released their first album before I had even learned to crawl or say my first word. Oi Polloi has since toured internationally, released over 30 albums, and two documentaries have been made about them. But most importantly, they have done all of this completely DIY. Thirty-one years later they are still touring and recording new albums. To this day, the do-it-yourself ethic is still the standing stone of their music. Credited with founding the sub-genre of Gaelic punk, these days Oi Polloi mostly sing in Scotch Gaelic, the traditional language of their culture, which they also use in their daily communication with one another. More than any other band, Oi Polloi epitomizes the ethics of DIY punk.

> Got our own bands our own scene
> our own values our own dream
> of creating an alternative

> to the shit of the music biz.
> (Oi Polloi, 2006)

I catch myself singing along to the chantey anthem styled lyrics, as fast, straightforward punk riffs accompany the words. While I could never choose a favorite from their hundreds of songs, this one stands out to me, as it depicts the culture of punk and why it means so much to those of us involved. Punk has always been more than just music and angst. Punk was about creating an alternative, building "a better world on the ashes of this one." (Profane Existence Magazine slogan). Punk was birthed from a rejection of a culture that rejected us, a culture that marginalized anyone who was different, or anyone who wanted something different. Something more: "Punk had originated as a statement, 'Do It Yourself': your own band, your own sounds, your own future" (Rimbaud 1998, p. 78).

Do-it-yourself means something special in its use within punk culture. Whereas in the consumer world of capitalist markets, DIY may refer to purchasing high end tools and specialty kits from the local hardware store or hobby shop, in punk culture it holds a different connotation. The sentiment of DIY is well-expressed by former political prisoner and animal activist Jake Conroy, saying,

> Myself and a friend started passing out information on animal rights and animal liberation at the local hardcore shows. We would be doing tables upwards of 3–4 times a week. There wasn't much in the way of ALF [Animal Liberation Front] support merchandise at the time, so we screened pro-ALF shirts and hoodies we got from the thrift store and sold them to cover the costs of photocopies. (Conroy, 2012, para. 4)

This helps build a culture where we are all equals because anyone can take part simply by taking initiative; "Band members were no different from the audience members both in beliefs and often skill as well" (O'Hara, 2001, p. 153). In this subculture, the shows are often set up not by professional promoters, but by bands or kids in the scene who keep the shows cheap, $4 or $5 at the door, so even the poor street kids can afford to go. The bands play for the cost of travel, the promoters don't keep a cent for themselves, posters are put up by hand, and security is done by the kids who attend the show. All of this works to keep costs down. Shows are often set up in people's basements, living rooms, or in local community halls instead of bars so that fans of all ages can attend. And the interviews are done not by music press, but rather by kids in the community who don't want to wait for someone else to hopefully ask their favorite band for an interview, so they do it themselves, asking the questions they want to hear answers to. Often those interviews are published in fan-zines (or zines), which are handmade magazines, reproduced on a photocopier. Oi Polloi's front man Deek Allen explains how much this has developed over the decades and how it has benefited the underground music scene:

> Now you've got this underground DIY network all over the globe, so if you want to be a band and to tour and release records, it's possible to do that to a large extent without ever having to deal with the corporate side of things. (Nattrass, 2012)

This culture of mutuality and self empowerment is built on the free labor of people all over the world, many of which are youth. All of this effort is because we believe a better world is possible, because we know that if we want an alternative to what we see as wrong with this culture, then we need to do the work to make it happen. No one else will do it for us. This is precisely why so many people active in DIY subculture rail harshly against bands who take the cultural capital we have created to sell it (or parts of it) to make personal profit, making money off our movement with no benefit to the DIY culture.

I THOUGHT IT MEANT MORE

> I thought it was a new way to live
> about creating an alternative
> to music business rock stars sitting backstage
> Pathetic sell-outs—where is the rage? (Oi Polloi, 2006)

Oi Polloi was part of a small community made up a handful of bands, many of which would go on to positively alter the communities they lived in and become legendary to future generations of punks—even if the majority of people in the rest of the world may never know their names. Few of those bands remain active today, and even fewer remain true to the ethics of DIY. In 1997, long time anarcho-punk band Chumbawamba signed to EMI, a major label with connections to the manufacture of nuclear arms. The following year Oi Polloi released this song as their response, complete with lengthy liner notes further detailing their position. Focusing on what the movement was meant to be, and what it meant to them, Oi Polloi pulled no punches in hiding their feeling of betrayal as Chumbawamba became one-hit-wonders touring the world and playing in front of corporate banners and speaking on daytime TV talk shows. The title of this song draws on the title of Chumbawamba's first album, *Pictures of Starving Children Sell Records*, as well as the cover art of their sixth album *Anarchy!*, which depicted a baby in the process of being birthed. Oi Polloi spins it around, throwing it back in their faces. Turning what was intended as a commentary on the profiteering of rock stars and charity organizations from the misery of children from war-torn nations into their own comment on how Chumbawamba have profiteered off of what was supposed to be a movement for social change. Chumbawamba quickly became known—not for their numerous albums or years of great music and lyrics that used humor and art to sharply criticize everything from voting to charity—but instead for a single pop song about a hangover. "There's that song, the one about getting knocked down and then getting back up again, but their body of work is like an iceberg; the bulk of it is submerged below the surface, difficult to get a hold of" (Smith, 2012). Meanwhile Oi Polloi continues to tour completely DIY spreading a message of "No compromise in defense of our earth!" an Earth First! slogan adopted by Oi Polloi. As Deek Allen explains,

> We don't of course mean that everyone should still be walking around with mohicans and dreads, clad in black rags held together with CRASS patches, at the age of 50 (though fair play to you if that's what you want to do!) but we'd like to see people holding true to their ideals and beliefs. The "punk" ideas inside the head rather than the hairstyle on top of it being, in our view, the most important thing. (Oi Polloi, 2006a, 2006b)

> Alice Nutter on T.V.?
> that's not a site that impresses me
> played last year at the big brewery show
> last year's Chumbas—this year's Kylie Minogue. (Oi Polloi, 2006)

NEVER GIVE IN

I grew up in a small town of 700 in the prairies. Kitscoty Alberta, named after a stone circle in Scotland, was known for three things: the golf course, the high school hockey team, and the enormously high suicide rates among teenagers. Every second year, two in a row would commit suicide. With 270 students ranging from grades 7–12, two every second year is a lot. School was hell for me. I was the most bullied kid in the entire town. Even the other bullied kids would make fun of me, in hopes they would deflect attention from themselves. The term "bullying" doesn't even begin to describe the harassment and violence that I experienced on a daily basis. I was regularly punched, kicked, spat on, called names, tripped, pushed, and my locker or book bag would be destroyed on a near weekly basis. On one occasion I physically had my pants torn off by a couple of kids a few grades above me. They laughed as I cried. More commonly I would get called "fag" and told I stunk. The teachers tended to be complicit, pretending to not notice what was happening right in front of their eyes. On occasion, they crossed the line from complicit to active involvement as they would mock me or call me names in front of the class, making fun of my hair or clothing.

Kitscoty was a hockey town, with a lot of money coming from the Alberta oil industry (the tar sands). Homophobia, racism, sexism, ableism, and classism were rampant. Of course I didn't know these words back then, but I understood the meanings all too well. I was a very small kid, with bifocal glasses, unable to catch or hit a ball, was poor at running, and came from a family with very little money. Most of my clothes came second hand in a school where branded logo t-shirts were a marker of economic status. At first I turned to self-destructive behaviors like cutting and burning myself, drinking and doing drugs. Seldom would a day pass where I did not think about suicide, or dream about the school burning down; anything to get me out of it.

It was at this point, around age 13, that I was first introduced to what might be called punk, and I honestly believe I would not be here today if I hadn't been. At first it was simply the rebellious imagery, fashion, and the disdain for "jocks" or "preps"—the children of the privileged—that I related to. Angry songs, mocking those kids who had physically, emotionally, mentally, and at times even sexually abused me. Punk gave me something to hold on to, a way to throw that scorn I had suffered back...rebellion. Punk also gave me an analysis of issues I would later come to know as class and capitalism and a framework to begin learning about a number of other struggles and issues. More importantly, every two-minute, three-chord song was a reminder that I was not alone. But the most important thing I took from punk was the DIY mentality.

Two months before my sweet 16, I left Kitscoty. For the first time I took my life truly into my own hands, as I hitchhiked across the country to Ontario. A year later I was a street kid, spiked Mohawk, studded leather jacket, panhandling for food and booze on Whyte avenue in Edmonton, Alberta. I lived communally in an abandoned building with 12 other street kids. Many of them had similar stories to my own. I learned a lot during that time, and it was during this time that I quit using drugs (other than alcohol and tobacco) and quit cutting and burning myself. Six years later I would go completely drug free, and I have been straight-edge and vegan ever since. Again, these choices were directly influenced by the liner notes and lyrics of various punk bands.

Punk put me on a path to action. By 2005, I was living on the west coast of the colonial nation state known as Canada, where I became active first in Food Not Bombs, cooking a vegan healthy meal out of donated food that we would give away for free every week. I had first heard of FnB back in 1996, in Edmonton's punk scene, where if you brought a vegan, non-perishable food donation for FnB, the door cost of the punk show would be a buck or two cheaper. Within a year of coming to the coast I was organizing punk shows for underground bands, starting when an older FnB organizer approached me asking if I would set up a benefit show for the local chapter. I had no clue how to do it, but I had a friend in a local band called Mechanichal Separation, so I asked her if they would play, and it all came together. Things spiraled from there. I became active in various campaigns, from anti-vivisection work with Stop Huntingdon Animal Cruelty, to fundraising for Amnesty International, and camping illegally as an act of civil disobedience to (successfully) challenge local bylaws that made it illegal for homeless people to sleep anywhere within the city limits. Over the years I worked with bands from all over the world. I set up talks and workshops for internationally known speakers and co-founded the Victoria Anarchist Bookfair.

REFERENCES

Conroy, J. (2012, November 15). Critique of "Do not support the ALF." *Because we must.* Retrieved August 9, 2013 from www.becausewemust.org/jake-conroy-shac-7-critique-of-do-not-support-the-alf/

Crass. (1983). *Yes sir I will* [Album]. London, UK: Crass Records.

Natrass, S. (2012). "Oi Polloi Interview with Deek Allen." No fun city zine. Victoria, CA: No Fun City Collective. Issue 3.

O'Hara, C. (2001). *The philosophy of punk: More than noise.* Oakland, CA: AK Press.

Oi Polloi. (2006a). *Total resistance to the fucking system.* [CD]. Duisburg, DE: Social Bomb Records. Back cover.

Oi Polloi. (2006b). Pictures of women giving birth sell records. On *Total resistance to the fucking system* [CD]. Duisburg, DE: Social Bomb Records.

Potter, W. (2011). *Green is the new red: An insider's account of a social movement under siege.* San Francisco, CA: City Lights Publishers.

Rimbaud, P. (1998). *Shibboleth: My revolting life.* Oakland, CA: AK Press.

Smith, A. L. (2012). *Chumbawamba's long voyage.* Retrieved August 9, 2013 from http://jacobinmag.com/2012/07/chumbawambas-long-voyage/

PART V

REPRESSION

CHAPTER 9

"STATE RUN RADIO" BY LUPE FIASCO

Andrew J. Ryan

You know music doesn't mean anything if we are not in step with the time in which we live.

—Minister Louis Farrakhan

INTRODUCTION

Wasalu Muhammad Jaco, better known as Lupe Fiasco, rose to prominence in 2006 with the release of his critically acclaimed album *Food and Liquor*. Raised Muslim, he initially disliked rap, a fact he shares on the track "Hurt Me Soul," "Now I ain't tryna be the greatest // I used to hate hip-hop... yup, because the women degraded // But Too $hort made me laugh // like a hypocrite I played it" (Jaco, 2006). Settling on poetry, Lupe Fiasco joined a group but quickly left due to the "gangster-based" lyrics he felt compelled to write in order to fit in.

As a solo artist, his remixes of Kanye West garnered the attention of industry insiders. Remixes, where an original song is reworked with new lyrics, have long been a staple of rap. Lupe's "Mohammad Walks," derived from West's "Jesus Walks" as well as "Conflict Diamonds," reworked from West's "Diamonds from Sierra Leone" brought accolades from established artists. In each song, Lupe displays noteworthy rhyme skills while sharing

Rebel Music, pages 81–92

knowledge with the listener. Kanye West eventually invited Lupe to rhyme on "Touch the Sky," a song from Kanye West's sophomore album, *Late Registration.*

Avoiding the downfall that entraps rising stars, Lupe Fiasco did not let mainstream success take him off message. Each of his albums contains exquisitely rhymed messages, explicit and veiled, meant to challenge the status quo of Hip Hop. In 2007, popular rapper Souljah Boy was quoted as saying "I don't want to be super-Lupe-Fiasco-lyrical and niggas don't know what the fuck I'm talking about" (HipHop DX, 2010). Lupe quickly responded with "Super Lupe Rap": "Soulja call it Super Lupe Lyrical // You can't understand me or mimic my miracles. // Imagine, an emcee being criticized for being too... um, intelligent" (Jaco, 2010).

At the time, Souljah Boy was one of the most recognizable names in Hip Hop, receiving airplay (buoyed by "Crank That") across the nation. He and other artists were keenly aware of radio stations' desire to play music that could be marketed to a broad fan base, often sacrificing lyrical content in the process. Through songs like "Dumb it Down," Lupe rails against radio-friendly, dumbed-down music lyrics, and in "The Real," he vehemently argues his music is meant to educate and not just entertain. Through his music, Lupe has been able to edu-tain (educate and entertain) audiences worldwide.

Seminal rap group EPMD famously called out artists who chased airplay over remaining true to their audience on the 1992 hit "Crossover." The song was a valiant attempt to remind consumers of rap's anti-establishment roots and to beware of artists who create pop and R&B sounding songs to sell records. One of the classic lines from the song as delivered by Erick Sermon:

> Changed up they style, from jeans to suits and
> Thinkin' about a pop record, somethin' made for the station.
> (Sermon & Smith, 1992)

Sermon is referencing the radio station, a key element in getting music to listeners.

Many rappers faced the choice between making profit and being a prophet. Said differently, do I attempt to make money or do I attempt to enlighten my audience? In the second verse, PMD states his preference:

> frontin on they fans, . . . saying
> "damn, it be great to sell a mill"/
> That's when the mind switch to the pop tip/
> (Kid, you're gonna be large!)
> Yea right, that's what the company kicks. (Sermon & Smith, 1992)

PMD offers a comical, yet somewhat realistic, relationship between the artist and the record company. As the artist ponders a pursuit of pop music stardom, the record company cheers them on: "Kid you gonna be large!" The insertion of the record companies' influence should not be lost. "Rapper's Delight" and the majority of rap's early hits were released on independent labels. The late 1980s and early 1990s saw many of these labels acquired by large record companies. In the process, these corporate companies asserted control of the content of the music.

On the track "State Run Radio," Lupe offers a treatise against the dominance of popular radio. He not only takes aim at radio stations but at the artists and the audience who eagerly devour any music put in front of them. In many ways, Lupe embodies the essence of author Molefi Asante Jr.'s definition of the post-Hip Hop generation:

> in search of a deeper, more encompassing understanding of themselves in a context outside of the corporate hip-hop monopoly.... Post hip-hop is an assertion of agency that encapsulates this generation's broad range of abilities ideals, and ideas, as well as incorporates recent social advances (i.e., the women's movement, the antiwar movement, gay rights, anti-globalization) that hip-hop has either failed or refused to prioritize. (Asante, 2008)

While the message is not entirely new, Lupe repackages it for a new generation. This chapter will examine Lupe Fiasco's "State Run Radio" against the literal and historical interpretation of "state run" urban radio.

THE HOOK—HOW THE RADIO MAKES MONEY

"State Run Radio" tackles the topic of mainstream radio's insistence on playing a limited number of songs each day. Radio stations aim to give their audience what they want and what is familiar. Rap and pop superstars earned their status from radio. Feeding their audience songs from recognized stars maintains their loyalty as listeners. Record labels supply songs to radio stations, assisting them to connect their artists to listeners. Recently, summer concerts promoted by radio station have served as another way to push artists on radio listeners. Quite often performers receive little or no payment for their performance in return for *support* from the radio station.

Radio stations generate revenue based on advertising. Rates for advertising are based on listenership, or the number of people who tune in each day. Due to their spending prowess, the youth and young adults demographic is especially sought after by advertisers. Capturing their musical tastes often means high revenues for a station. The balance of appeasing their audience while wooing advertisers leaves little room for introducing new or risqué artists to receive airplay. The chorus of "State Run Radio" speaks to the limited rotation of songs played.

> You must be,
> a radio station
> And who are we, we must be
> A number one song, spinning all day long And over again,
> And over again, And over again, And over again, And over again
> And we know when, When we call in,
> And nothing's free,
> Sounds to me like.
> (Jaco & Manzoor, 2011)

He ends the hook with a reference to radios` giveaways. In these promotions, listeners vie for a prize. Unbeknownst to most contest winners, the prizes are taxed—sometimes up to 50% of their value. *Hence, "nothing is free."* Lupe employs the poetic device of repetition to drive home his point, repeating the phrase "*Sounds to me like, State run radio*" *eight* times and reinforcing the repetition of songs: "*And over again. And over again.*"

VERSE 1

Lupe begins the verse by announcing an interruption to the broadcast. As his name suggests, he is causing a fiasco, in this case against the status quo.

> The future's cloudy and it's raining on the poor class,
> The roads to peace are closed, and the traffic's on the war paths.
> (Jaco & Manzoor, 2011)

Without mincing words, he attempts to enlighten the radio listenership to what is going on. Lupe intelligently keys in on the poor (lower) class, often the primary audience of urban radio. While rap songs with harsh messages about violence and drugs are often referenced, few focus on positive tracks.

> Love is balling on a budget
> the military says It's gon' need more cash, →
> to keep fighting for your gas. Keep us in our hoods.
> (Jaco & Manzoor, 2011)

Showing his range, he borrows a phrase, "Ballin on a Budget" from Teck, cast member on MTV's Real World Season 8. Repurposing the phrase with the word "love" and segueing into the catastrophic cost of war reminds the listener of Lupe's intellectual range. Born in 1982, Lupe has seen no fewer than three wars in his lifetime. Moving from war to education, Lupe postulates about the impact of education and its ability to shrink the mindset of youth.

> ... and hope we never explore pass, Stay inside of your half
> believe the lies you learn in your class.
> (Jaco & Manzoor, 2011)

While a great equalizer for some, education, especially in poorer areas, does little to emancipate the mindset of students. While every neighborhood has its dark places, rarely are the positives mentioned—"that's there's no treasure in your trash." In commending the work of West coast Hip Hop activists in his book *Hip-Hop Matters: Politics, Pop Culture and the Struggle for the Soul of a Movement*, Watkins (2005) asserts:

> For all of the hype about Hip Hop's grandiose presence in pop culture, or its presumed negative impact on youth behavior and values, few people acknowledged the extent to which it has enhanced, enlarged, and empowered the views and voices of young people. (Watkins, 2005, p. 185)

Though Michelle Malkin, Juan Williams, John McWhorter, and others speak of the negative influence of rap, few look for evidence of the good it inspires. Lupe's song attempts to wean the audience off of the negative and toward something better.

Lupe, speaking directly to the listeners, continues to shape their mindsets. The "escapist" nature of rap can allow for fantasy to become reality: to leave poverty through music. Lupe rails against songs with uninspiring lyrics being played on the radio:

> And the ceiling has the same feeling, That the floor has,
> and that's where you should stay, This is what they play.
> (Jaco & Manzoor, 2011)

On 2007 song called "Dumb It Down," Lupe confronts the reality gap in rap music. The hook contains a fictional radio executive stating what Lupe (using the abbreviated version of his name, Lu) Fiasco's music is doing to listeners, followed by a suggestion to "Dumb it Down!"

> You've been shedding too much light Lu (Dumb it down)
> You make 'em wanna do right Lu (Dumb it down)
> They're getting self-esteem Lu (Dumb it down)
> These girls are trying to be queens Lu (Dumb it down)
> They're trying to graduate from school Lu (Dumb it down).
> (Jaco, 2007)

Further, Lupe comments on the imbalanced reality that mainstream radio fosters. Songs performed by millionaires, absorbed by those without such means, yet intended to alleviate the wealth gap between audience and listener. In his essay, "Hip-Hop Turns 30, Watcha Celebratin' For?" Greg Tate (2004) argues that "hiphop floats through the virtual marketplace of branded icons as another consumable ghost, parasitically feeding off the host of the real world's people—urbanized and institutionalized—whom it will claim till its dying day to 'represent.'" Tate, like Lupe, takes rap music to task for failing to represent the very audience that created it as he writes, "hiphop is money at this point, a valued form of currency where brothers are offered stock options in exchange for letting some corporate entity stand next to their fire."

This form of hegemony is powerful in dumbing down knowledge and awareness. In attempting to bring a more realistic view of issues, Lupe, perhaps coincidentally, summons Brazilian educator Paulo Freire's notion of conscientization, where after politicizing social issues results from dialoguing, critical consciousness is raised, which inspires action.

SECOND VERSE

The second verse begins with Lupe questioning the motives of mainstream radio. He argues that by listening to "weak" lyrics, the audience is kept in its place.

> You're now tuned into the weakest,
> Frequency of fear, keep you locked right here.
> (Jaco & Manzoor, 2011)

Historically, there was a time when finding positive music on the radio was commonplace. Music historian Nelson George writes,

> Radio has historically been so intimately connected with the consciousness of blacks that it remained their primary source of entertainment and information well into the age of television. Even in today's VCR and CD filled era, black radio plays a huge role in shaping black taste and opinion—when it remembers its black audience. (George, 1988)

The fact is, rap was never part of Black radio's message; it was primarily R&B music.

Initially hailed as party music, Grandmaster Flash and the Furious Five changed rap forever with the release of "The Message." Released in 1984, the song documents the struggles, trials, and tribulations many inhabitants of the Bronx experience. The mid-to late eighties saw a rise in conscious rap, with artists such as Rakim, KRS-One, and newcomer Queen Latifah bringing messages of empowerment and political activism to their music. Nationalistic groups like X-Clan, Jungle Brothers, and Public Enemy weaved social commentary with their music. This period was likely the high point for popular rap that had a message.

Nineteen-ninety saw the introduction of parental advisory labels to rap albums. Reality-challenging albums by Public Enemy, KRS-One, Ice Cube, and others carried a government warning, paving the way for safer rap acts. Soon, pop acts like DJ Jazzy Jeff and the Fresh Prince, MC Hammer, and Vanilla Ice shot to the forefront without any semblance of a social message.

> And hope you never leave this, never be a leader
> Think inside the box, and follow all procedures.
> (Jaco & Manzoor, 2011)

Taking the message out of rap changed the listening experience. The education part of *edutainment* was missing. During this period, the emergence of Soundscan, a digital system to count and track CD sales, provided economic incentive for stations to play rap. A few rap stations began to appear, often the result of format changes. These stations would be strongly positioned to benefit from the gold rush rap was soon to unveil, while Black radio lagged behind. Today, it's not uncommon to see competing rap stations in a single city, unheard of in the 1990s.

Despite rap's success, the establishment in Black radio was able to keep rap from penetrating the R&B charts. As late as 1996, rap records would consistently be near the top of the Billboard charts but non-existent on R&B charts. Unlike the Billboard pop chart, the R&B charts were still calculated on a word of mouth system, which was subject to bias and manipulation. Without digital tracking, R&B reigned supreme.

The unwillingness to support rap was not held by all. Legendary DJ, after whom Sylvia Robinson named "Rapper's Delight," commenting on the lack of an organizing place for rap in 1999 stated, "I said, they deserve a break too. Are you going to be prejudiced toward somebody because you have a form of music that you don't understand or you don't like. These are brothers! Let the kids make some money" (Spady, Lee, & Alim, 1999, p. 352).

Rap with a softer message was becoming a cash crop for radio but left a void for artists who did attack the status quo. In a section titled "Careers over Activism," Kitwana, former *The Source* editor, attempts to diagnose the political apathy in Hip Hop:

> [popular culture] where young Blacks, mostly professional entertainers and athletes, gain wide visibility by association with corporate products. As activists concerns generally run counter to corporate interests, today's young Black

> professional artists maintain a code of silence when it comes to political issues. (Kitwana, 2003, p. 151)

If they were to get paid, sacrifices were to be made.

Lupe implores listeners to find something different, to resist being dependent being fed the same songs (over and over). In closing the verse, Lupe pretends to be a caller to a radio station:

> Hi, you're on the air, now what you want to hear?
> Well we ain't got the truth, but how about a remix?
> Different is never good, good is only what we pick,
> You ain't got a hit, unless it sounds like these did.
> (Jaco & Manzoor, 2011)

Instead of asking for a song, he asks for the truth. Unfortunately, the truth isn't in normal rotation, so he asks for a remix. Noting the economic realities of truth, Lupe challenges the radio's determination of what makes a "good" song—the oft sought after "radio friendly" hit. Sadly, what makes a song a hit is often based on its resemblance to other hits. Being too smart on a song may alienate an audience. Jay-Z, who helped Lupe secure a music deal, addresses the matter on "Moment of Clarity"

> I dumb down for my audience
> And double my dollars
> They criticize me for it
> Yet they all yell "Holla."
> (Carter, 2003)

Jay-Z recognizes his quixotic critics who seemingly love his music, "Yet they all yell 'Holla.'" As of 2013, Jay-Z has recorded 15 studio albums with 11 of them reaching number one on the U.S. Billboard chart.

THIRD VERSE

In the final verse, Lupe leaves the listener with a warning to not only pay attention to what is being played, but what's *not* making it on the airwaves—namely the uplifting/positive songs. Independent artists, who aren't bound by contractual agreements and a need to make money for their record label, aren't heard. Much of this is due to radio's insistence on playing what is popular to keep advertisers coming back. Also not getting played on the air is truth, with Lupe using simile to compare it to the United States embargo against liquids (shampoo) on an airplane.

As Lupe speaks about mainstream radio, it can be argued, rap's grittiness can be attributed to radio ignoring their initial existence. While "Rapper's Delight" was a huge hit in 1979, it didn't open the floodgates for others. Disco was still king. As calls of "disco sucks!" gained momentum, it created a void in the charts. In the first half of 1979, the Billboard R&B chart shared nearly 50% of the records listed on Billboard's pop single chart. By fall 1982, only 17% of songs were on both lists. Rap never stood a chance of being played when traditional genres weren't being played.

College radio stations embraced early rap. Spared from corporately controlled playlists and given freedom of expression, shows like Columbia University's *Stretch Armstrong & Bobbito Show* provided an unfiltered brand of rap where the deejay controlled the content. Deejays on large radio stations don't have that luxury.

Playing songs from unsigned or local talent offers little return for investment from advertisers, the listening audience, or the established record labels. Thus, many radio stations have limited playlists—often deferring to established stars. In 2003, Washington DC Hip Hop station WPGC fired deejay Peter Rosenberg for saying "DC radio sucks" in an interview. He continues: "It's just impossible for [non-major-label talent] to get into rotation around here" (Daly, 2003). Rosenberg would get the last laugh as several years later he became a radio fixture at Hot 97 in New York City, earning a reputation for his high Hip Hop IQ.

> Propaganda's everywhere, constantly on replay
> All the hits all the time back to back on relay.
> (Jaco & Manzoor, 2011)

Lupe ends by comparing the onslaught of songs with vacuous meanings to radio propaganda. In the United States, the use of music as propaganda goes back to World War II. Voice of America was created by the United States to espouse American values in foreign countries. Once the war ended, there was great debate over continuing its existence. Eventually, the U.S. Information and Educational Exchange Act of 1948 (also called the Smith-Mundt Act) was passed, which authorized the United States Department of State to broadcast to foreign countries during peacetime. The bill was amended in The Foreign Relations Authorization Act of 1972, which made it illegal for U.S. broadcasters to transmit "information about the United States, its people, and its policies" prepared for foreign audiences—essentially State -run radio.

There are documented examples of radio as propaganda. An August 19, 1958 headline of the *Evening Independent* offers the following headline: "America Plans Propaganda U.S. Radio to Reach Arabs." The article discusses budget appropriations made to set up a radio station to counter Radio Cairo in Egypt (Allen, 1958).

In the 1960s, jazz was used as a weapon in the Cold War. An April 30th, 1966 *New York Times* headline reads: "Soviet Poets fail to Captures Dakar: Duke Ellington the Winner in Propaganda Skirmish." Kofsky (1970) writes, "[Jazz] is utilized for Voice of America broadcasts, its practitioners are eagerly sought for State Department Tours" (p. 112). He further comments on the fact that Duke Ellington (who, by the way, is the most covered jazz artist in history) was denied a Pulitzer prize in music the year before, "[this] exemplifies the unwritten rule that jazz may be eminently serviceable for cold war campaigns abroad, but when it comes to winning acceptance at home, the prospects are more grim" (Kofsky, 1970, p. 112). In many ways, Kofsky could be talking about Hip Hop as well. Despite nearly 40 years of existence, Hip Hop's acceptance as art has been slow.

In 2005, youth in the suburbs of Paris staged a prolonged riot aimed at drawing attention to their skyrocketing unemployment and the lack of action from government. French law dictates radio to play at least 40% of their songs in French during prime hours. As a result, authentic French rap has a means to reach the masses. Several French politicians claimed that the messages of rap helped incite the riots. A bill was drawn up to make it illegal for songs to criticize the government. Though the measure was never passed, it demonstrates what can happen when access to the airwaves isn't restricted by corporations.

> We're really where it lives, make 'em hear the records we play,
> Build your own station, become your own DJ.
> (Jaco & Manzoor, 2011)

Similar to the youth in France, in the final bars Lupe asks his listeners to take an active role in the music they choose to listen to. Lupe asks the audience to use the Internet to make their own radio stations. In doing so, they would be able to control the content of their musical selections. This idea was initially espoused by Public Enemy front man Chuck D in 1999, telling *Rolling Stone* magazine: "Digital distribution levels the playing field" (Goodman, 1999, para. 11). Chuck D foresaw the benefits of the Internet when it came to artist royalties as well as making it easier for artists to reach consumers. It should be noted that the iTunes store was not even created until 2003. Chuck D was ahead of his time.

CONCLUSION

Author Thomas Chatterton Williams (2010) argues that Hip Hop culture and rap music almost sent him on a spiraling path toward failure. In his book, *Losing My Cool: How a Father's Love and 15,000 Books Beat Hip Hop Culture*, he argues that the music of his youth has few redeeming qualities and should be blamed for many of the ills facing urban youth today. In the penultimate chapter, the author, now in graduate school in Washington DC, recalls the moment rap stopped informing him. "I couldn't do it, not once I actually had some philosophy under my belt and was getting in the habit of thinking for and informing myself" (Williams, 2010, p. 181).

Chicago-bred emcee Lupe Fiasco would likely agree with him, except he chose to do something about it. In the summer of 2010, rising megastar Rick Ross released "B.M.F. (Blowing Money Fast)." The song, an ode to Atlanta-based crime cartel Black Mafia Family (BMF), became one of the summer's most played tunes. Borrowing the idea from Washington DC based rapper Day-One, Lupe Fiasco remixed the song, calling out the names of famous Black leaders instead of convicted criminals. The track, "BMF (Building Minds Faster)," gained attention on the Internet, though it never reached mainstream status.

Lupe Fiasco's suggestion of another outlet to get music should not be taken lightly. In 1992, bell hooks warned:

> There is a direct and abiding connection between the maintenance of white supremacist patriarchy in this society and the institutionalization via mass media of specific images, representations of race, of Blackness that support and maintain the oppression, exploitation and overall domination of all Black. (p. 2)

It may not be State-run radio, but it's a far cry from people-run radio, where deejays decided the playlist. Aided by the Internet, consumers now have more options. Challenging the listener to be proactive, on the last bar of the track, Lupe implores, "Build your own station, become your own deejays" (Jaco & Manzoor, 2011).

REFERENCES

Allen, R. S. (1958, August 19). America plans propaganda—U.S. radio to reach Arabs. *The Evening Independent.* Retrieved from http://news.google.com/newspapers?nid=950&dat=19580819&id=PgNQAAAAIBAJ&sjid=VlUDAAAAIBAJ&pg=2601,2840160

Asante, M. K. (2008). *It's bigger than hip-hop: The rise of the post-hip-hop generation.* New York, NY: St. Martin's Press.

Carter, S. (2003). Moment of clarity [Recorded by Jay-Z]. On *The black album* [CD]. New York, NY: Def Jam Records.

Daly, S. (2003, March 14). Pop secret. *Washington City Paper.* Retrieved from http://www.washingtoncitypaper.com/articles/25796/pop-secret

George, N. (1988). *The death of rhythm & blues.* New York, NY: Penguin Group USA.

Goodman, F. (1999, March 9). MP3 technology poised to redefine music industry. *Rolling Stone.* Retrieved from http://www.rollingstone.com/music/news/mp3-technology-poised-to-redefine-music-industry-19990309

hooks, b. (1992). *Black looks: Race and representation.* Brooklyn, NY: South End Press.

Hip-Hop DX. (2010). Soulja Boy Takes A Shot At Lupe Fiasco? Retrieved June 21, 2013 from http://www.hiphopdx.com/index/news/id.12871/title.soulja-boy-takes-a-shot-at-lupe-fiasco

Jaco, W. M. (2006). Hurt me soul [Recorded by Lupe Fiasco]. On *Lupe Fiasco's Food & Liquor* [CD]. Chicago, IL: 1st and 15th Entertainment.

Jaco,W. M. (2007). Dumb it down [Recorded by Lupe Fiasco]. On *Dumb it down* [CD]. New York, NY: Atlantic Records.

Jaco, W. M. (2010). Super Lupe rap [Recorded by Lupe Fiasco]. On *Pre-Lasers* [CD]. Retrieved from http://www.datpiff.com/Lupe-Fiasco-Pre-Lasers-mixtape.184251.html

Jaco, W. M. (n.d.) BMF (building minds faster). http://www.okayplayer.com/news/Audio-Lupe-Fiasco-B_M_F-Building-Minds-Faster.html

Jaco, W. M., & Manzoor, D. (2011). State run radio [Recorded by Lupe Fiasco]. On *Lasers* [CD]. New York, NY: Atlantic Records.

Kitwana, B. (2003). *The hip hop generation: Young blacks and the crisis in African American culture.* New York, NY: Basic Civitas Books.

Kofsky, F. (1970). *Black nationalism and the revolution in music.* New York, NY: Pathfinder Press.

Sermon, E., & Smith, P. (1992). Crossover [Recorded by EPMD]. On *Business never personal* [CD]. New York, NY: Def Jam.

Spady, J. G., Lee, C. G., & Alim, H. S. (1999). *Street conscious rap.* Philadelphia, PA: Black History Museum.

Tate, G. (2004, December 28). Hiphop turns 30—whatcha celebratin' for? *The Village Voice News.* Retrieved August 23, 2013 from http://www.villagevoice.com/news/0501,tate,59766,2.html

Watkins, S. C. (2005). *Hip hop matters: Politics, pop culture, and the struggle for the soul of a movement.* Boston, MA: Beacon Press.

Williams, T. C. (2010). *Losing my cool: How a father's love and 15,000 books beat hip-hop culture.* New York, NY: Penguin Press.

CHAPTER 10

"IRON FIST" BY GOLDFINGER

Ed Avery-Natale

Goldfinger is a punk rock band that formed in Southern California in 1994 and gained some national success with their song "Here in your Bedroom" from their 1996 self-titled debut album. In many ways, "Here in your Bedroom" is a quintessential representation of Goldfinger in their early days (Feldman, 1996). The song's themes, all links to various forms of identification, emphasize heterosexual love and romance and personal introspection. These are the dominant themes in Goldfinger's music from their founding until their 2002 album *Open Your Eyes.*

The very title *Open Your Eyes* hints at the shift that Goldfinger makes with this album. While their first three albums contained almost no hint of a political identification for the band (though heterosexuality can certainly be understood as a politicized identification), the 2002 album contains some blatantly political messages alongside their more traditional songs. Thus, the phrase "open your eyes" should be interpreted in various ways. By using the word "your," they are clearly identifying anyone who purchases the album, presumably their fans; they are instructing their fans to open their eyes to the world around them. However, due to the highly introspective nature of their lyrics generally, we should also assume that the title addresses the band

Rebel Music, pages 93–100

as well. In this way, the album's title informs us of the identification transition that takes place here in the themes of some of the songs on the album.

Goldfinger's lyricist and front man, John Feldmann, admits that this record marks a departure for the band. In an interview with the website "In Music We Trust," he says that in the three years since the band's previous album he had come to identify strongly with animal rights and that he wants to use his position as the leader of a band to address these concerns because "I realized that people will listen if I'm on stage singing about it" (Steininger, 2002). Even the cover of the album reflects these concerns, as it shows a young punk standing in front of a wall with his eyes closed. Behind him are a series of posters advertising milk and beef as well as cigarettes and beer, while also telling people that they need to lose weight. The implication of the image is if people would "open their eyes" they would see the horrors being committed in the world around them, something that the band has presumably done leading up to this album.

With the song "Spokesman" they criticize advertising and the media, emphasizing the ways in which these structures alienate us from our desires by creating our tastes for us. However, this is only the beginning of the political themes on the album. With the title track, "Open Your Eyes," the band directly addresses animal rights for the first time, referencing "shots to the head" of animals, and telling their listeners to:

> Open your eyes
> To the millions of lies
> That they tell you everyday
> Open your mind
> To the clever disguise
> That the advertisements say
> (Feldmann, 2002a)

Similarly, in the song "FTN" (which stands for "Fuck Ted Nugent") they sing:

> Fuck Ted Nugent
> he's a fucking jerk
> I wish that he'd be gone
> Chauvinistic Republican, kills animals
> (Feldmann, 2002b)

The song also goes on to criticize the National Rifle Association then Jennifer Lopez for using animal products in her clothing, makeup, and food. The band claims that they play this song at every concert and that Feldmann gives a speech about why he is vegan before doing so in order to both "entertain and educate" fans (Steininger, 2002).

All of this is clearly linked to the band's evolving identification as a politically-minded group dedicated to animal rights. The themes are both social and personal, and this is a necessary element of any identification. Identification theories tell us that all identification narratives are socially structured in discourse but are also personally incorporated into the narrative of the subject through interpolative processes. Therefore, we should not be surprised here that the personal issues of diet and politics are equally social; these are issues that are, after all, deeply social *and* deeply personal.

Understanding these changes that the band went through is important if we hope to also understand how they came to write a song like "Iron Fist." The themes analyzed above increase on their following album, 2005's *Disconnection Notice*, which continues to include political themes with an emphasis on animal rights. Like *Open Your Eyes*, the album's title is again meant to convey the message that will be included in the more political songs on the album. The title *Disconnection Notice* is clearly a theme linked to identification and expresses a disconnnection from society at large, which Feldman links to his diet. If we understand society and the nation that one lives in as an identification ("I'm American," or "I'm a part of modern society"), then becoming alienated, or disconnected, from this society also means identifying with the counter-hegemonic trends that seek to change the very society one is disconnecting from. As Foucault tells us, any hegemonic power structure also brings with it a counter-hegemonic power seeking to alter that system. Each of these is a part of a dialectical identitarian conflict seeking to maintain or produce a particular mode of power. Here, Feldman is telling us that he has come to identify with a counter-hegemonic structure.

This counter-hegemonic identification is reflected in many of the songs on *Disconnection Notice*, such as "Behind the Mask" and "Iron Fist." In the latter song the band attempts to paint a personal picture of the ramifications of their alignment with a counter-hegemonic ideology and identification, an identification that includes the opposition to the oppression of animals. The song depicts an individual, having participated in some sort of radical action, being attacked by the police. The police raid the protagonist's house while he is "asked a million questions." It is also in "Iron Fist" that we begin to get a better understanding of the band's continuing political development and the ways that Feldmann has become more disconnected from the world around him and in which he lives. Early in the song, he sings:

> This morning I was dreaming of angels
> Covered in the warmth of their wings
> This morning was a different lifetime I've come to believe
> (Feldmann, 2005)

Here we can interpret "this morning" as metaphorically representing a "different lifetime," much like the different approach that Goldfinger has taken to music and politics represent different lifetimes for the band.

We also see more of an existential conflict for Feldman in "Iron Fist." In this song we see a series of existential and identitarian struggles confronting the protagonist of the story, who we can suspect represents Feldmann himself and his disconnection from the world around him. We can first understand with the line "I thought they were democratic, not an iron fist" that he is stating a previous belief in democratic governance, a belief that is challenged by the police and other authorities' response to the protagonist's protest actions. We see that this belief has changed when he says that he had "been trained to respect them" but has since seen that they only serve "the wealthy," indicating that the system under which he lives is plutocratic rather than democratic.

These are all, ultimately, themes linked to identification. Firstly, the narrator is engaged in a struggle that maps onto the struggle between the hegemonic system, represented by its repressive and ideological state apparatuses, and the counter-hegemonic structure. In "Iron Fist" we see that the narrator was trained to respect the system and the police, presumably through schooling and other functions of the ideological state apparatus. However, as Althusser (1971) tells us to expect, once the narrator has come to identify with a counter-hegemonic subjectivity, the repressive state apparatus (the police and so on) intervenes with force. This puts the narrator into an existential crisis: does he reject his identification with American hegemonic ideals, thus altering his identitarian plot, or does he reject the ethical ideals that have become central to his sense of self?

This is a significant existential and identitarian theme and connects to the title of the album, as the narrator is reflecting on his separation, or disconnection, from the nation-state. The protagonist of the story finds that if he does what he is told by the authorities, then he may be able to maintain his allegiance to his country, but to do so he would have adhere to what he knows is wrong. The next line indicates that he has made his choice and that, in practice, there was never a choice at all. He says that the country of his birth was built upon treason and slavery, indicating that he could never side with this, as doing so would transgress his ethical ideals. Presumably, we can see the term "slavery" as having two meaning, referencing both African slavery in the American South and the slavery of animals in contemporary factory farms.

Ultimately, that the protagonist would pick this side is inevitable due to the line that tells us that he knows the nation's side is "wrong." Taylor (1989) tells us that, as humans, we construct our identitarian life narrative forms in which we almost always orient ourselves toward a subjective, but nonetheless meaningful, conception of "the good."

> We cannot but orient ourselves to the good, and thus determine our place relative to it and hence determine the direction of our lives, we must inescapably understand our lives in narrative form, as a "quest" ... because we have to determine our place in relation to the good, therefore we cannot be without an orientation to it, and hence must see our life in story. (Taylor, 1989, pp. 51–52)

Therefore, in the narrative of "Iron Fist," the protagonist, knowing what is "wrong," has little choice but to side against his nation and with those it oppresses, such as non-human animals. To do otherwise would violate the ethically guided narrative function of identification. That this would happen is particularly significant for political punk rock. As I have shown elsewhere (Avery-Natale, 2012), many anarchist-punks are deeply dedicated to an identification that is linked to ethics and maintaining a narrative in which they are doing what is subjectively understood as "right." While it is unclear whether Feldmann would identify as an anarchist, he clearly has come to identify with several elements of far-left ideologies, including a radical interpretation of animal rights, and therefore we might expect that he too will have invested in this identitarian ethical plot.

What we can see from all of this is Goldfinger's, and especially Feldmann's, continuing political development into a more politically identified band and individual. "Iron Fist" outlines Feldmann's alienation, or disconnection, from the world in which he lives, thus granting the album its title. He has put his fans and others on notice that he is disconnected, and "Iron Fist" indicates to us that there is no turning back from this point. While Goldfinger may never be a wholly political band, we can presume that from this point onward, they will never be a non-political band again either. Their identitarian plot has shifted in a decidedly political, and perhaps radical, direction. In doing so, their plot shift has produced an existential and identitarian dilemma of feeling disconnected and alienated from their country of birth and the hegemonic systems that organized their former plot, and as such their former characters and narratives (Vila, 2000). This conflict is resolved in a new alignment with social struggle, thus resolving the need to restore the band's, and Feldmann's, identification. In other words, in properly Deleuzian language, they had identified with a particular territorialization, the hegemonic foundations of America and capitalism, but their coming radicalization forced them into a deterritorialization, a line of flight, as the hegemonic system did not allow for their new identitarian plot. Therefore, and as Deleuze and Guattari (1980) tell us to expect, they reterritorialized onto another surface: the counter-hegemonic struggle against the system that they had been raised to respect.

IDENTITARIAN CONCLUSIONS

There are a number of identitarian conclusions that can be drawn from this analysis. First, we can see that the narrative nature of identifications functions not only in the stories that we tell about ourselves in our day-by-day lives, but also in the songs that we write, and presumably in other works of art. In narrative identification theories, it is argued that we as human beings understand our selves and construct our various identifications in a "storied" format (Ochberg, 1994; Richardson, 1990), that our life experiences are organized into narratives with particular characters and events, and that all of this is structured by the plot by which we understand our lives progressing (Vila, 2000). Above we saw that Goldfinger, with their album *Disconnection Notice*, went through a particularly significant plot shift as they came to identify with a counter-hegemonic discourse.

In going through this plot shift, we should expect that particular "things" took on different meanings, and this plays out in the song "Iron Fist." For example, the meaning of America, democracy, slavery, the police, and even right and wrong took on dramatically different meanings. These are all "things" that existed in the world for Goldfinger prior to the plot shift, but the discursive meaning of these things changed. This tells us something important about the nature of identifications in relationship to "reality" as well. In short, there is a physical world out there, but it does not have axiomatic or "true" meaning. Instead, meaning and truth are functions of discourse. Therefore, the particular discourses that we invest identitarian meaning into will produce different interpretations of the world; America is no longer democratic, the police are no longer your friends, and animals are no longer there to be your slaves.

Secondly, we see the significance of ethics to identifications. As I stated above, Charles Taylor (1989) argues that human beings usually narrate our existence toward "the good," meaning that which is culturally and subjectively constructed as a positive outcome; in other words, most people are the protagonists of their own story. While historically ethics were understood as an objective truth (for example, in the works of Plato and Aristotle, it is argued that "the good life," from which their ethics are derived, was by definition the mastery of the self and the dominance of reason over desire), this idea has been challenged in contemporary philosophy. This is most obvious in the work of Michel Foucault who, borrowing from Nietzsche, contrasts ethics with morality (Foucault, 1990; Moore, 1987). Similarly, Sartre has claimed that our ethics are based on our absolute freedom, not from an outside force such as god(s). For Sartre, it is only through human freedom that our actions become ethical or unethical.

The essential consequence of our earlier remarks is that man is being condemned to be free.

> We are taking the word "responsibility" in its ordinary sense as "consciousness (of) being the incontestable author of an event or of an object."... But in addition the situation is *mine* because it is the image of my free choice of myself. (Sartre, 1956, p. 815)

Furthermore, for Sarte this "absolute freedom implies absolute responsibility" (Plantings, 1958, p. 245), and in "Iron Fist" we see the repercussions of this responsibility. The narrator of "Iron Fist" clearly believes that he *could* choose to invest in the hegemonic rather than counter-hegemonic discourse. His ability to do so is properly Sartrean, as Sartre believed that we are free to choose what we are, and that even those things that limit us, what Sartre called "facticities," are a function of this choice and the identifications that produce our desires. However, to do so in this case would produce an ethical dilemma. The narrator of "Iron Fist," as Sartre implies, "carries the weight of the whole world on his shoulders; he is responsible for the world and for himself as a way of being." Therefore, unless the narrator wants to slip into an instance of Sartrean bad faith, he must choose to take responsibility for the world and, in this case, the animals living in it. To do otherwise would put him back on the side of the "iron fist" of capitalism, industry, and the state.

REFERENCES

Althusser, L. (1971). Ideology and ideological state apparatuses. In L. Althusser, *Lenin and philosophy and other essays.* New York, NY: Monthly Review Press.

Avery-Natale, E. (2012). *Narrative identifications among anarcho-punks in Philadelphia.* (Doctoral Dissertation, Temple University). Retrieved from http://digital.library.temple.edu/cdm/ref/collection/p245801coll10/id/174972

Deleuze, G., & Guattari, F. (1980). *A thousand plateaus: Capitalism and schizophrenia.* New York, NY: Continuum.

Feldman, J. (1996). Here in your Bedroom [Recording by Goldinfger]. On *Goldfinger* [CD]. New York, NY: Universal.

Feldmann, J. (2002a). Open your eyes [Recorded by Goldfinger]. On *Open your eyes* [CD]. Santa Monica, CA: Mojo.

Feldmann, J. (2002b). FTN [Recorded by Goldfinger]. On *Open your eyes* [CD]. Santa Monica, CA: Mojo.

Feldmann, J. (2005). Iron fist [Recorded by Goldfinger]. On *Disconnection notice* [CD]. Los Angeles, CA: Maverick.

Foucault, M. (1990). *The history of sexuality: Volume 1.* New York, NY: Vintage.

Moore, M. C. (1987). Ethical discourse and Foucault's conception of ethics. *Human Studies, 10*(1), 81–95.

Ochberg, R. L. (1994). Life stories and storied lives. In A. Lieblich & R. Josselson (Eds.), *Exploring identity and gender. The narrative study of lives* (Vol. 2, pp. 113–144). Thousand Oaks, CA: Sage Publications.

Plantings, A. (1958). An existentialist's ethics. *The review of metaphysics, 12*(2), 253–256.

Richardson, L. (1990). Narrative and sociology. *Journal of contemporary ethnography, 19,* 116–135.

Sartre, J. P. (1956). *Being and nothingness.* New York, NY: Pocket Books.

Steininger, A. (2002). New album, new label, new Goldfinger. *In Music We Trust.* Retrieved from http://www.inmusicwetrust.com/articles/48h04.html

Taylor, C. (1989). *Sources of the self: The making of modern identity.* Cambridge, MA: Harvard University Press.

Vila, P. (2000). *Crossing borders, reinforcing borders: Social categories, metaphors, and narrative identities on the U.S.-Mexico border.* Austin, TX: University of Texas Press.

PART VI

EXPRESSION

CHAPTER 11

"FIGHT FOR YOUR RIGHT" BY BEASTIE BOYS

Daniel White Hodge

If Run-DMC took Hip Hop to the edge of suburbia during the 1980s, then the Beastie Boys drove it straight into the heart of strip malls and gated communities. The Beastie Boys represent one of Hip Hop's first white, articulate, punk, funk, rock, rap groups who were not only concerned about Hip Hop's sustainability—as we would later learn—but were also a strong identifying factor for white, rebel, Gen-X, punk, 1970s and 1980s youth. They represented a slice of the urban community that very few people, in mainstream America, had been privy to or had knowledge of. This slice of white American youth, which the Beastie Boys connected with so well, were, as Eminem would later remind us, displaced, marginalized, disenfranchised and also a bi-product of Reagan's neglected middle class who too, were forgotten and left to the wayside with Blacks, Latinos, and poor Asians. The Beastie Boys not only represented this swatch of youth and young adults but would remain a Hip Hop classic group with songs such as: "No Sleep Til Brooklyn," "Paul Revere," "Brass Monkey," "So What'cha Want," and of course "Fight For Your Right." These songs connected with people in many ways. For one, they resonated with the context they were sung in: the tumultuous 1980s (see Chang, 2005; Kitwana, 2003). Second,

Rebel Music, pages 103–110

these songs contained a rebellious attitude and worldview that many within the Gen X generation could identity with and relate to as a generation who felt—by and large—neglected and overlooked (Hip Hop's roots were very firmly planted in giving people voice, see Rose, 1994). Third, these songs represented a voice, a voice of an often overlooked class of people in the U.S.: the poor, working class, white family. Lastly, these songs set the stage for artists such as Nirvana to build on what Beastie Boys laid out as issues during this time.

Thus, the Beastie Boys were more than just a "rap group." They were more than just a group of loud, obnoxious, white "boys." Originally formed as a four-piece hardcore punk band in 1981 by Michael Diamond (vocals), John Berry (guitar), Adam Yauch (bass) and Kate Schellenbach (drums), the band appeared on the compilation cassette *New York Thrash,* before recording their first EP "Polly Wog Stew" in 1982. After achieving moderate local success with the 1983 experimental Hip Hop 12-inch "Cooky Puss," the group transitioned to Hip Hop in 1984 and released a string of successful 12-inch singles. They were a group to which many were able to relate, particularly with their dress, attitude, music video designs, and overall persona. The Beastie Boys came up in a time when America was at a low point economically, rap was in its teens, and when Hip Hop culture was beginning to take the stage as a force to be reckoned with (Chang, 2005).

The song "Fight for Your Right" was an instant identifier for the Beastie Boys. Released on their album *License to Ill* (1986), it reached number seven on the Billboard 100 the week of March 7, 1986 and was later named one of the Rock and Roll Hall of Fame's 500 songs that shaped Rock and Roll. The album cover had an American Airlines Boeing 727 crashing into the side of a mountain with the album title on the tail wing. The song, in reality, was a parody on the "party life" of the 1980s and intended to make fun of such hit songs such as Mötley Crüe's "Smokin' In The Boys Room" and Twisted Sister's "I Wanna Rock"—which were hit songs describing and glorifying party life. But, as time would tell, the parody and irony were lost with most listeners, and the song was labeled as a "party type" song. Mike D commented that

> the only thing that upsets me is that we might have reinforced certain values of some people in our audience when our own values were actually totally different. There were tons of guys singing along to "Fight for Your Right" who were oblivious to the fact it was a total goof on them. (MTV interview, 1995)

So, if that was the case, what made the song so popular and a classic?

Let us answer that by first looking at the song itself and then investigating the factors in the song that gave and continue to give it such an appealing identity element. First, the song is a seemingly simple three verse song with a chorus. Yet, the words are what make this a powerful track and create such an everlasting space to create meaning. We have to remember that words do not contain their meanings; people do. In other words, there is the literal dictionary meaning of a word, but that is little to no consequence to someone who attains meaning, identity, and worth from it in a different manner. Therefore, the song opens with a verse almost every tween, teen, and young adult can relate to, "You wake up late for school—man you don't wanna go" (Yauch, 1986). Right off, the Beastie Boys set the tone for what the song is going to be: connecting with, identifying in, and engaging the rebellious part of our selves, and where better to start with than school.

This is similar to what researchers call cultural identity salience—the strength of affiliation we have with larger cultural associations, in this case rap music (Ting-Toomey, Yee-Jung, Shapiro, Garcia, Wright, & Oetzel, 2000). The Beastie Boys capitalize on this by grabbing the listeners ears on issues most young people have with school. This sets the tone for the entire song, which is to rebel against what current society thinks, prescribes, illuminates, creates, and / or tells one to be. The Beastie Boys create—albeit in an unplanned manner—a worldview that rebels against current societal trends and continues the youth revolt that preceded Gen X. In music, there is a chance to identify with something that is both larger than you but is still you (see Hodge, 2009). Tricia Rose, Hip Hop scholar and cultural critic, reminds us that "Hip Hop emerged as a source for youth of alternate identity formation and social status in a community whose older local support institutions had been all but demolished along with large sectors of its built environment" (Rose, 1994). And with the growing visibility of Black youth and culture during the 1980s, "Fight For Your Right" was an anthem, of sorts, for those not only in the Hip Hop generation to identify with, but also those outside of it in other musical genres and culture (e.g., rock, metal, punk) (Kitwana, 2005).

The rest of the first verse engages these issues surrounding school, parents, and an educational system that is not relatable. The Beastie Boys assert:

> You ask you mom, "Please?"—but she still says, "No!"
> You missed two classes—and no homework
> But your teacher preaches class like you're some kind of jerk (Yauch, 1986)

Then end the first verse with the pronounced chorus: *You gotta fight* [guitar swing] *for your right* [guitar swing] *to party!* (Yauch, 1986).

As Mike D commented, the irony of the actual genesis of the song gets lost. But, what emerges is an anthem of sorts for youth to embrace as a way to point the middle finger at society. The cajoling rhymes, which are filled with parodies, truth, comedy, and powerful wordplay, create an atmosphere that listeners want to take part in. A large part of the attraction to "Fight for

Your Right" is the infusion of all those things (comedy, truth, wordplay) and the seriousness of the group in real life to issues such as war, poverty, and injustice. The Beastie Boys took stances around the issues of justice, activism, and peace. They were artists who lived the messages they discussed in their music and used their public profile to push that agenda for good. For example, the band performed three concerts (in Los Angeles, New York City, and Washington D.C.) to raise money for the Milarepa Fund and dedicated the royalties from "Shambala" and "Bodhisattva Vow" from the *Ill Communication* album to the cause. The Milarepa Fund aims to raise awareness of Tibetan human rights issues and the exile of the Dalai Lama. In 1996, Yauch organized the Tibetan Freedom Concert, a two-day festival at Golden Gate Park in San Francisco that attracted 100,000 people. The band increased its level of political activism after the September 11, 2001 attacks, organizing and headlining the New Yorkers Against Violence Concert in October 2001. Funds from the concert went towards the New York Women's Foundation Disaster Relief Fund and the New York Association for New Americans (NYANA). At the 1998 ceremony, Yauch addressed the issue of Muslim people being stereotyped as terrorists and declared that most people of the Muslim faith are not terrorists. These comments were made in the wake of the U.S. Embassy bombings that had occurred in both Kenya and Tanzania only a month earlier. At the 1999 ceremony in the wake of the horror stories that were coming out of Woodstock '99, Adam Horovitz addressed the fact that there had been so many cases of sexual assaults and rapes at the festival and the need for bands and festivals to pay much more attention to the security details at their concerts. These are merely a few examples of the lived life of activism and justice that the Beastie Boys stood for.

The next verse opens with the parental frustration so many adolescents feel, especially as it pertains to societal deviant behavior such as porn, smoking, and illicit sex. The second verse is:

> You pop caught you smoking—and he said, "No way!"
> That hypocrite—smokes two packs a day
> Man, living at home is such a drag
> Now your mom threw away your best porno mag (Bust it!) (Yauch, 1986)

As you look at this simplistic four line verse, it tells a narrative that is multifaceted, having universal appeal and showing complexity in its nature toward life. Once again, with cultural identity salience the strength comes by affiliation: the affiliation to the words and the meanings created around them. Therefore, the Beastie Boys generate this world of problems, struggles, and issues surrounding adolescence life. What makes it more unique is that it is done so simplistically. They, in essence, call out the double standards, hypocrisies of society, duplicities, and ironies much of American culture embraces—whether they realize it or not (e.g., "family values" but many U.S. families have to work fifty to sixty hours a week negating "family time" for career; "moral values" yet women are paraded as sex objects and used to sell almost anything in mainstream media). The verse creates space for the listener to agree and nod their head to seemingly "dumb" and "stupid" social mores we follow without ever thinking twice.

Moreover, what the Beastie Boys do in verse two is to complain in a way that makes sense to the listener and context. They ask the very poignant question: Why should I follow the "rules" if you yourself are not going to either? As such, the Beastie Boys call out the sexual repression America has dealt with since its inception by making a reference to their "best porno mag."

In these spaces, a type of social identity formation is made—one that is also connected to urban or, as Murray Forman (2002) describes, "symbolic meaning of 'inner city.'" In this space, boundaries are pushed, the issues of urban life are engaged with, and the permission to be angry, upset, and even enraged is granted. These create discourse markers and allow the listener to mark their experiences with the song. The urban flavor of rap music and Hip Hop culture is a universal appealing form for youth—especially white youth. The "ghetto" feel to the music and rebellious attitude that it percolates with is also an identifying factor. Even the term "inner city" is a powerful way to connect with people. Once again Forman states, "... in its symbolic representational forms, the term has a resonance that reaches through the urban cores and the suburban and non-urban sectors of society, cutting to the very heart of the contemporary body politic" (Forman, 2002). The Beastie Boys, in one short verse, create this space and, as time would prove, created a song in which many were able to engage and embrace as their own in an almost neo-spiritual way (see Hodge, 2010). More importantly, they wear geographical identifiers that also create identity in the listeners: in the video a red shirt that shows the neighborhood name Stuyvesant (which also has the word "leader" in the center) in north-central Brooklyn is a clear urban geographical marker, which Forman discusses as important, for those living on the East Coast, particularly New York, to identify with.

In the last verse, which follows the almost identical rhythmic chorus, the Beastie Boys verbalize their disgust with rules, traditional social mores, and parents who do not understand. The last verse states:

> Don't step out of this house if that's the clothes you're gonna wear
> I'll kick you out of my home is you don't cut that hair
> Your mom busted in and said, "What's that noise?"
> Aw, mom you're just jealous—it's the Beastie Boys! (Yauch, 1986)

Here, the Beastie Boys begin to connect the dots to what Bakari Kitwana refers to as the alienation of white youth in the 1980s. Here, parental disconnect, abandonment, the intolerance to loud music were all covered. Kitwana (2005) explains this further:

> First and foremost among the reasons white kids love Hip Hop is the growing sense of alienation from mainstream American life they experience in the 1980's. As the 1970's turned into the 1980's and America moved into what was billed as a new economy, Americans, regardless of race and class, began to feel increasingly uncertain. The generation of white kids [generation X] was confronted by socioeconomic issues that alienated them from mainstream as well. (pp. 23–24)

The Beastie Boys' appearance in the video to this song reinforces the class they are representing: middle to lower class. And even though there are gold medallions worn, one of the medallions is an old Volkswagen symbol that appears to have been taken off an automobile (also very common in the 1980s, especially with Mercedes Benz). Thus, the connection here to what Kitwana is describing.

The Beastie Boys end with a shout out to themselves in response to the loud noise question. They assert their "fight" with loud noise, long hair, and clothes that do not fit with the Boomer generation's mode of thought. Young people from around the world are able to identify with this "fight" and connect with the even larger question of "what next?" Young people that were interviewed for a different project commented on how the Beastie Boys shaped and influenced their lives: "I think shit, if they are able to talk about stuff nobody else is, so can I. They helped me in better understanding what it means to be a white, broke ass, male living in this country. Shit, there is fight; a fight for our own identity in America, ya feel me?" (Hodge, 2010, pp. 54–55).

The Beastie Boys' style and sense of fashion arguably set fashion trends. Their use of gold medallions, Adidas sportswear, and skinny style jeans set trends for decades; principally for white, punk, rebellious youth. The video of "Fight for Your Right" illustrates the uptight, conservative, and conformist parents who have children that are the same way—but secretly, as the end of the video would reveal—want to "party." The video, which was also reexamined in 2011 in a short film entitled *Fight for Your Right Revisited*, demonstrates the desire to rebel and call out the double standards of society—especially within the context in which the Beastie Boys found themselves in.

What I have been arguing here is musical identity formation. It is a strong connection to the music, artists, and context in which it takes place. The Beastie Boys set a standard and were one of the first white rap and punk fusion groups to take the stage at a time when rap was still in its initial stages. "Fight for Your Right" was a song that created a space for white youth—lower middle class and disenfranchised—to find some meaning in their world. While the song was not intended to be a "party" type of song, rather a parody of that lifestyle, the meanings derived from the song went far beyond what the group could have even hoped for. This song was a thematic song with which other young people were able to connect and feel like their voice was being heard in the public sphere.

It is worth mentioning that there are other elements assigned to this song and rap group, such as race. Kevin Powell, journalist and cultural critic, said in a *Newsweek* interview in 2003, "Let's be honest. All this fascination with Hip Hop is just a cultural safari for white people" (cited in Kitwana, 2005). And it has been noted that the Beastie Boys were able to say the things they were able to say because of white privilege while other groups such as Public Enemy (who were on the same label for a while) were slammed for their messages on injustice, racism, and social inequality (see Kelley, 1994). While the scope of this chapter did not permit the further discussion of these matters, these too are identification factors in which people find their identity. As a note, the Beastie Boys were featured on the cover of *Beyond Race* magazine for the publication's summer 2007 issue. The Beastie Boys have continually been cited as a white band that has consistently gone beyond conventional musical stereotypes.

Lastly, with the death of Adam Yauch (MCA), fan outcry from Black, Latino, Asian, and white was clearly abundant. And, in their induction into the Rock and Roll Hall of Fame in 2012, the sentiment was still apparent for what the Beastie Boys had established with their song "Fight for Your Right"; clearly it is a song that people will identify with, well into the 21st century. Yauch's passion and talent for filmmaking led to his founding of Oscilloscope Laboratories, which in 2008 released his directorial film debut, the basketball documentary *Gunnin' For That #1 Spot* and has since become a major force in independent video distribution, amassing a catalogue of such acclaimed titles as Kelly Reichardt's *Wendy and Lucy*, Oren Moverman's *The Messenger*, Banksy's *Exit Through The Gift Shop*, Lance Bangs and Spike Jonze's *Tell Them Anything You Want: A Portrait Of Maurice Sendak*, and many more. Under the alias of Nathanial Hörnblowér, Yauch directed iconic Beastie Boys videos including "So Whatcha Want," "Intergalactic," "Body Movin, and "Ch-Check It Out." Under his own name, Yauch directed 2011's *Fight For Your Right Revisited*, an extended video for "Make Some Noise" from Beastie Boys' *Hot Sauce Committee Part Two*, starring Elijah Wood, Danny McBride, and Seth Rogen as the 1986 Beastie Boys, making their way through a half hour of cameo-studded misadventures before squaring off against Jack Black, Will Ferrell, and John C. Reilly as Beastie Boys of the future. The legacy of Beastie Boys will continue, and their music will forever be a part of the rich legacy of Hip Hop culture.

REFERENCES

Chang, J. (2005). *Can't stop won't stop: A history of the hip hop generation.* New York, NY: St. Martin's Press.

D, Mike. "Beastie Boy Relfection." MTV (1995).

Forman, M. (2002). *The 'hood comes first: Race, space, and place in rap and hip-hop, Music/Culture.* Middletown, CT: Wesleyan University Press.

Hodge, D. W. (2009). *Heaven has a ghetto: The missiological gospel & theology of Tupac Amaru Shakur.* Saarbrucken, DE: VDM Verlag Dr. Muller Academic.

Hodge, D. W. (2010). *The soul of hip hop: Rimbs timbs & a cultural theology.* Downers Grove, IL: InterVarsity Press.

Kelley, R. D. G. (1994). *Race Rebels: Culture, Politics, and the Black working class.* New York, NY: Free Press.

Kitwana, B. (2003). *The hip hop Generation: Young Blacks and the crisis in African-American culture.* New York, NY: Basic Civitas.

Kitwana, B. (2005). *Why white kids love hip-hop: Wankstas, wiggers, wannabes, and the new reality of race in America.* New York, NY: Basic Civitas Books.

Rose, T. (1994). *Black noise: Rap music and Black culture in contemporary America.* Middletown, CT: Wesleyan University Press.

Ting-Toomey, S., Yee-Jung, K., Shapiro, R., Garcia, W., Wright, T., & Oetzel, J. G. (2000). Cultural/ethnic identity salience and conflict styles in four U.S. ethnic groups. *International Journal of Intercultural Relations, 24,* 47–81.

Yauch, A. (1986). (You gotta) fight for your right (to party) [Recorded by Beastie Boys]. On *Licensed to ill* [CD]. New York, NY: Def Jam/Columbia.

CHAPTER 12

"TERMINAL PREPPIE" BY DEAD KENNEDYS

Kirby Pringle

When I was twelve years old I bought my first LP record at Music Plus in the Northridge Mall (in the San Fernando Valley), where I asked for the new self-titled *Suicidal Tendencies* album. They were out of it. However, a blondish female store clerk cheerfully told me in a manner signaling that I was lucky, "Oh, but we have the Dead Kennedys!" I had heard that name somewhere. I picked up the album—frightening in and of itself—but not in the ghoulish heavy metal way. The cover displayed a stark black-and-white photograph taken during the Ugandan famine of a starving child's hand being grasped by a larger adult white hand whose palm was facing the viewer. It was just two hands, with "Dead Kennedys" scrawled in crayon above, nothing else.

The record was titled *Plastic Surgery Disasters*. At home sitting down at my turntable, and with trembling hands, I put the needle down. The album spoke to me quite literally. The intro opened with a woman's voice, jubilant and with perfect diction, speaking above some disjointed, trashy—almost, dare I say, jazzy—dissonant noise. This unpleasant intro warned me against aspiring to becoming a preppy as it begins, "Why are you such as a stupid asshole? Would you really like to know?" (Biafra, 1982a). After this "public service announcement" comes the music, a blistering barrage of hardcore punk rock.

Rebel Music, pages 111–119

The Dead Kennedys were one of the most popular punk bands on the West Coast. They were best known for the lyrics and political antics of front-man Jello Biafra, who, for instance, unsuccessfully ran for mayor of San Francisco in 1980. But the band also had a member that was one of just a handful of African Americans to be on stage in punk rock, D.H. Peligro. He was the band's drummer beginning with *Plastic Surgery Disasters* and played on "Terminal Preppie."

Plastic Surgery Disasters, released in 1982, was two years old by the time I first discovered it. The record is generally considered the Dead Kennedys' best album. Several of the thirteen songs attacked what was unquestionably deemed the best option for a white middle-school student like me: that is, to stay in school, do what I was told, go to college, fall in love, defer to specialists (as in shrinks or PhDs), and when I got older, to vacation in a recreational vehicle (RV).

The song that is the best lyrically, in my opinion, is "Terminal Preppie" (Biafra, 1982b). In typical punk fashion, a lyric sheet was provided with the LP, only the Kennedys also included a booklet with their iconic collage-style art. The "Terminal Preppie" page showed the dark side of college life, such as a girl popping a pimple on her breasts. Despite being replete with references from the early 1980s, the song is still relevant today. The preppy (I will use its common spelling with a "y") is a phenomenon that still exists—just go to Stone Harbor or Cape Cod, and you will witness upper class elites—usually white—wearing Ralph Lauren Polo shirts, Top-Sider shoes, pleated Docker shorts, and webbed belts. Their conversation, at least for the men, usually concerns three things: stock portfolios, college football, or golf, just as it has always been and will continue to be.

Preppies originated from English preparatory high schools that were popular among the wealthy in the eighteenth and nineteenth centuries but have since gone out of favor due to the educational strategies of individualism (as opposed to group character), the advent of the automobile, and a declining birth rate among the English (Leinster-Mackay, 1984). Prep high schools in America are mainly an East Coast phenomenon, although West Coast schools did exist, such as the Belmont School near San Francisco, that were based on the prep model from Britain. These prep schools guaranteed entrance into the "right" college, which in America could mean an Ivy League school. A new student enrollment in the 1950s exploded at prep schools due to the nation's prosperity, changing test standards at colleges (partly because of the baby boom and the G.I. Bill), and a fear of Soviet advances in science and technology exemplified by the launching of the Sputnik satellite. Prep high schools in America such as the prestigious Hill School in Pennsylvania saw, for instance, 743 applicants for only 130 places in 1960 (Powell, 1996).

The Kennedys (the royal political family, not the band) were the ultimate preppies and popularized the leisurely college lifestyle in the 1960s. *Preppy: Cultivating Ivy Style,* a book that was outsourced and printed in China much like preppy garb is today, was authored by two preppy fashion designers who wrote:

> When the youthful Senator John F. Kennedy of Massachusetts became President of the United States in 1960, he brought a whiff of Ivy with him to the white House—not only in his personal style, but also with his Harvard-educated coterie of advisors, all of whom wore classic American, natural-shouldered suits, horn-rimmed glasses and repp ties. (Banks & La Chapelle, 2011, p. 76)

The latter diagonally striped ties were started by Brooks Brothers in the 1920s and were based on British regimental or club ties, only the stripes were reversed. Jacqueline Kennedy, the First Lady, also sported a European-designed version of casual preppy style that was emulated by many impressionable American women (Banks & La Chapelle, 2011, p. 67, 77–78).

Thus it is no surprise that a band named the Dead Kennedys would pen a song called "Terminal Preppie." Where specifically did the inspiration for this song come from? The band could have certainly witnessed preppies in the San Francisco area where the band hails from. For instance, the first yacht club in the city was organized in 1867 (Mayo, 1998). However, it is evident that the song took most of its themes from a popular book published in 1980 called *The Official Preppy Handbook* written by Lisa Birnbach. A book originally meant to satirize the lifestyle, it was so dead-on that it was adopted as the Bible by preppies themselves with an extremely expensive hardcover special gift edition published that one could present to the family matriarch.

The Official Preppy Handbook is hilarious—sometimes unintentionally. To show the direct influence it had on the song, here are a few passages that helped create the lyrics of "Terminal Preppie" (Biafra, 1982b). The song begins, "I go to college that makes me so cool..." (Biafra, 1982b). Compare that to *The Official Preppy Handbook*:

> Generally, college is an occasion to be with other Preppies, whether they are from your Prep school, from your rival schools, or simply passing for Prep. Except for the minimal forays into scholarship, you enjoy an uninterrupted stream of parties, rather like a four year debutante season. But then again, as any self-respecting Preppy will tell you, college is just another Prep club itself. (Birnbach, 1980, p. 90)

The song continues, "I live in a dorm and show off by the pool" (Biafra, 1982b). Again, compare that to *The Official Preppy Handbook,*

> Residence is very important to your collegiate well-being. First and foremost you want to be always near campus in case an impromptu party pops us. There are those who would stray to off-campus apartments but they are not Prep and never will be. Secondly, the dorm room assigned to you by the housing office should quickly become a Prep palace. (Birnbach, 1980, p. 90)

The rest of the song very much follows the themes of *The Official Preppy Handbook.* Being a songwriter myself, my guess is that the Dead Kennedys singer Jello Biafra bought the book and found it an amusing parody of this elite group. He closely read the book, took a few pages of notes, and from those notes he compiled a song. Several of the lines don't quite rhyme but somehow follow a rhyming scheme as the words sputter by (just say these lines fast, and you will see what I mean):

> I join the right clubs just to build an impression
> I block out thinking it won't get me ahead
> My ambition in life is to look good on paper
> All I want is a spot is some big corporation.
> (Biafra, 1982b)

Punk rock is rife with criticisms of America's corporations—the engine that brings us the American Dream. Unlike most other political punk bands, such as those inspired by Crass in the UK that were quite direct by using slogans or theories, the Kennedys confronted different aspects of corporate America more personally, often through sarcasm, and especially on their first few records. Where "Terminal Preppie" diverts from *The Official Preppy Handbook* is evident in a few of the names mentioned, such as Springsteen, presumably Bruce Springsteen, a singer who is not particularly known as a favorite of preps, like say Donna Summer or Frank Sinatra.

The other name mentioned in the song is John Belushi, for instance, "John Belushi is my hero I lampoon and I ape him" (Biafra, 1982b). Comedian and actor John Belushi was apparently a fan of punk rock, having helped produce songs for the Los Angeles punk band Fear after having gotten them to appear live on *Saturday Night Live* (where the band's fans trashed the set). Amazingly, Belushi, who had been one of the two Blues Brothers with Dan Aykroyd, traded in his blues records, reportedly saying in September of 1981, "All I'm going to listen to is Fear and the Dead Kennedys" (Pisano & Colby, 2005, p. 242). If anything is not obvious to listeners today of "Terminal Preppie," it would be how big a star Belushi was when the song was released, a fact that was obscured by his tragic death. In January 1979, he was at his peak with the top late night TV show (*Saturday Night Live*), the number one selling album as part of the Blues Brothers, and the highest grossing comedy film of 1978 with *Animal House* (Pisano & Colby, 2005). One of the scriptwriters of *Animal House* remembered that the original treatment for the movie attempted to describe the shift beginning with the Kennedy assassination in 1962 and continuing through the free speech, civil rights, and anti-war movements when "fraternities were becoming increasingly marginalized as students converted their anarchic energy to legitimate political protest and activism" (Miller, 2006, p. viii). The line in the song about him is difficult to decipher but seems to indicate that John Belushi was a hero to preppies. Perhaps preppies imitated his drinking antics from both the film and in real life—think "Toga! Toga!" But Belushi's wild frat boy character in *Animal House* was essentially anti-prep; his fraternity was the rival to the Omegas, who were made up of upper class preps and debutantes. So perhaps the meaning is that Belushi was a hero to preps though he was challenging them.

The next line of the song relates to sports. However, differing from the song, Birnbach in *The Official Preppy Handbook* makes the point that preppies love a party (are alcoholics) and enjoy the revelry of sporting events but are usually not very knowledgeable about sports, which can be interpreted to imply that they wouldn't read a sports magazine. Though granted, they might know more about sports than current events. The song's line reads, "My news from the world comes from *Sports Illustrated*" (Biafra, 1992b). Sports are integral to the preppy. Football, according to *The Official Preppy Handbook* is okay to watch at a stadium but not to play, though the partying and complex rules make for confusion (Birnbach, 1980). The sports chosen by preps, to play at least, were usually tied to the country club: golf, or more English games like soccer and rugby, or squash, lacrosse, and rowing (Birnbach, 1980).

Historically much of the fashion of preppies originated with elite sports where the rich could show social standing and group affiliation. As James Mayo showed in his study of country clubs: "the foxhunter, tennis player, yachtsman, or polo player had to be appropriately dressed, so did the spectator" (Mayo, 1998, p. 50). Perhaps the best quote comes from a book authored by two prep clothing designers, enlightening in that it was written to celebrate prepdom, but most punk rockers would find this origin story a bit alarming:

> Preppies origins are rooted in the grounds of elite Ivy-League universities of the 1920s, where WASPy and wealthy gentlemen invented a relaxed new way for collegians to dress by co-opting athletic clothes from the playing fields, mixing them with genteel classics, and decking them out with caps, ties, pins, and other regalia to signify membership in a prestigious club or sport. (Banks & La Chapelle, 2011, p. 3)

Tennis, an exclusive sport in the nineteenth century, was particularly integral to the Preppy way of life. A French tennis champion, Rene Lacoste, nicknamed "Le Croc," invented a lightweight cotton piqued collared shirt in the 1920s with short-sleeves and a long tail on which he had embroidered a crocodile since that was his nickname—the predecessor to the polo shirt that so characterized the prep by the 1950s (Banks & La Chapelle, 2011, p. 49–50).

The Dead Kennedys promoted absurdist fashion; for instance, early photos of the band members showed all of them wearing black ties and a white dress shirt with a large, crude, spray-painted "S" across it to look like a dollar sign. Going beyond mocking preppy dress norms, at times they actually spoofed punk rock fashion by posing in leather jackets with unthinkable band names and logos on them, such as "Dolly Parton." To paraphrase their drummer D.H. Peligro, the band decided to wear pencil-thin mustaches and soul patches for their entire second U.S. tour after they noticed this new look was very irritating to their audiences (Peligro, 2013, p. 103).

Again, partying is integral to the leisure lifestyle of the preppy. Biafra (1982b) writes in the song,

> I'm proud of my trophies like my empty beer cans
> stacked in rows up the wall to impress all my friends.

In *The Official Preppy Handbook*, one section describes getting kicked out of school that suggests one method is to stack up so many Budweiser cans that the dorm room inspector won't be able to open the door (Birnbach, 1980, p. 69). In another section titled "Transforming the Dorm Room," number two on the list is "Beer cans, empty." Interestingly, number 29 is "Expensive stereo system reflecting your interest in technology not music" (Birnbach, 1980, pp. 92–93), somewhat similar to the Kennedys' "Holiday in Cambodia" song from their first LP: "play ethnicky jazz to parade your snazz on your five grand stereo" (Biafra, 1980). To finally emphasize that preps are anti-intellectual, Biafra writes in the song,

> No, I'm not here to learn . . .
> I just want to get drunk
> and major in business
> and be taught how to fuck
> Win! Win! I always play to win
> Wanna fit in like a cog in the faceless machine.
> (Biafra, 1982b)

The Official Preppy Handbook recommended staying away from majors such as philosophy and linguistics. They may not be more work than English or history, but they "smack of an equally undesirable effort: thought" (Birnbarch, 1980, p. 91). Stockbroker, account executive, investment banker, along with rancher, but only if the ranch is several hundred acres, are a few acceptable occupations allowed for preps. According to the book, maintaining preppyness depends on upholding the "safeguards of tradition" (Birnbarch, 1980, p. 78). Heritage is a core value—in fact, Polo by Ralph Lauren and other such standard preppy fare is referred to by clothing designers as "heritage wear" for its unchanging fashion quality and its unwavering support for the status quo that is projected upon its consumers. A large part of the competitiveness of preppies on the athletic field is preparation to thrive in the business world: "Wall Street, in the courtroom, at the club" (Birnbarch, 1980, p. 60). The final stanza of the song very much speaks to the preppy code of ethics, if one could call it that:

> I want a wife with tits, who just smiles all the time
> In my centerfold world, filled with Springsteen and wine
> Some day I'll have power. Some day I'll have boats
> A tract in some suburb with Thanksgivings to host.
> (Biafra, 1982b)

Again, the above lyrics of the song relate directly to *The Official Preppy Handbook*: the wet t-shirt contest, and enthusiasm shown by girls always saying "cute" and other superlatives (Birnbach, 1980, pp. 112, 217). The line about "my centerfold world" may be inspired by the wedding ritual when the morning after everyone flips to the newspaper to see what coverage it received (Birnbach, 1980, p. 178). A house in the suburbs is expected once hitting the age of thirty. "Some day I'll have power" from the song relates to the country club where one finds the Old Boy Network (Birnbach, 1980, p. 190) and corresponds to one of my favorite lines from the book: "You may want to be on the historical society and zoning board of your town, at least long enough to win permission to add that family room to your 1740 farmhouse" (Birnbach, 1980, p. 189).

Preppyism is a celebration of leisure, wealth, and power. The leisure being derived from the wealth, the power being derived from the subversion of democracy with the wealth, which is passed from Mummy and Daddy. At the center of the celebration is inheritance or "intergenerational wealth," as it is called. Robert K. Merton coined the term the "Matthew Effect" to explain why the rich get richer and the poor get poorer. This inherited advantage, he showed, can be described as compound interest that grows over generations, and is the looming reason that many African American families, who essentially started out with nothing in our nation's history, have been unable to invest or build home equity (Rigney, 2010). Another example is those students (like me) who were forced to take out loans for undergraduate and graduate school, which sometimes can top $100,000. The cycle is perpetuated when they have little money to make any substantial investments, unlike other graduates whose tuition was fully paid (via intergenerational wealth) and know that an inheritance also awaits (Marger, 2002, p. 39).

As the polar opposites, and thus mortal enemies, it is surprising that there were not more punk rock lyrics aimed specifically against preppies. Perhaps that is because most preppies did not know they were preppies. Before *The Official Preppy Handbook* spent 38 weeks at number one on the *New York Times* bestsellers list and was reprinted 41 times, the preppy's code was very much secret. Being the status-quo-maintaining elite in the backroom, preppies never worked hard to become self-reflective enough to raise an awareness of their culture.

Very aware of its punk culture, the Dead Kennedys album was also successful, as a landmark album that established the band as one of America's premier hardcore punk rock bands and gave a voice to youth that challenged the allowed aspirations as early as middle school. By the age of sixteen I had internalized the punk rock "do-it-yourself" spirit and had begun to play in my own bands, talent still lacking but youthful energy abundant. In fact, I dropped out of high school at fifteen (and only returned to school ten years later) to tour with numerous bands and reach other anti-preppy youth.

I had the opportunity to meet the Dead Kennedys singer Jello Biafra in 1989 outside of small show in Berkeley, California. I told him that it was his album *Plastic Surgery Disasters* that had convinced me to become a punk rocker—even getting a Mohawk at age twelve. Biafra simply replied, "Thank you. We worked really hard on that record."

REFERENCES

Banks, J., & La Chappelle, D. (2011). *Preppy: cultivating ivy style.* New York, NY: Rizzoli.

Biafra, J. (1980). Holiday in Cambodia [Recorded by Dead Kennedys]. On *Fresh fruit for rotting vegetables* [LP, Cassette]. San Francisco, CA: Alternative Tentacles.

Biafra, J. (1982a). The voice of Christmas past [Recorded by Dead Kennedys]. On *Plastic surgery disasters* [LP, Cassette]. San Francisco, CA: Alternative Tentacles.

Biafra, J. (1982b). Terminal preppie [Recorded by Dead Kennedys]. On *Plastic surgery disasters* [LP, Cassette]. San Francisco, CA: Alternative Tentacles.

Birnbach, L. (1980). T*he official preppy handbook.* New York, NY: Workman.

Leinster-Mackay, D. (1984). *The rise of the English prep school.* Philadelphia, PA: The Falmer Press.

Marger, M. N. (2002). *Social inequality: Patterns and processes.* Boston, MA: McGraw Hill.

Mayo, J. M. (1998). *The American country club: Its origins and development.* New Brunswick, NJ: Rutgers University Press.

Miller, C. (2006). *The real Animal House: The awesomely depraved saga of the fraternity that inspired the movie.* New York, NY: Little, Brown and Co.

Peligro, D. H. (2013). *Dreadnaught: King of afropunk.* Los Angeles, CA: A Barnacle Book.

Pisano, J. B., & Colby, T. (2005). *Belushi: A biography.* New York, NY: Rugged Land.
Powell, A. G. (1996). *Lessons in privilege: The American prep school tradition.* Cambridge, MA: Harvard University Press.
Rigney, D. (2010). *Matthew effect: How advantage begets further advantage.* New York, NY: Columbia University Press.

PART VII

RESPECT

CHAPTER 13

"DEAR MAMA" BY TUPAC SHAKUR

Marcella Runell Hall

I may not change the world but I guarantee that I will spark the mind that will.
—Tupac Shakur

The first time I heard "Dear Mama" in early 1995, I was a nineteen-year-old sophomore in college, living right outside of New York City. I was a longtime Hip Hop head, but only a moderate fan of Tupac; my geographic loyalty was with the Notorious B.I.G., or Biggie, as I typically still refer to him. However, "Dear Mama" (Shakur, 1995) was a game changer for me in every sense of the word. In previous songs Tupac had made respectful and even somewhat remorseful references to his mother, former Black Panther Afeni Shakur, but this was a complete, transparent homage to her struggles and celebrations as a single parent, and I was mesmerized from the first time I heard it. In fact, seventeen years later, it is still such a powerful classic Hip Hop text chronicling the group identity and experience of Hip Hop culture that I am using it in my work as a scholar and activist, most recently in my work with high school students incarcerated at Riker's Island.

Rebel Music, pages 123–129

WHO WAS TUPAC?

Tupac Shakur is perhaps one of the most fiercely contradictory and controversial figures in both U.S. history and Hip Hop culture, whose work has been the sole subject of academic conferences, books, essays, and debates. For many in my generation, Tupac, who was murdered more than fifteen years ago, was an influential icon. Named for an Incan revolutionary who led a pivotal uprising, he too sparked enthusiasm and controversy and wanted to create social change for marginalized people. He was also an artist wrought with contradictions, and "Dear Mama" presented fans with just that type of juxtaposition, on an album with other songs such as "If I Die 2Nite," "Lord Knows," "Outlaw," and "F*#!The World."

His mother, the subject of the beloved and renowned "Dear Mama," was a former Black Panther, a well-known activist, and a community leader with strong Black liberation political convictions and a network of Black activists whom Tupac knew and learned from. However, Afeni later became a recovering crack addict who struggled to make ends meet and at one point had to leave Tupac with a close family friend because she could not take care of him (Dyson, 2001; Guy, 2004).

Tupac, born in Harlem, New York, spent time attending a privileged performing arts high school in Baltimore, Maryland. He later became the most famous face of the East/West Coast Hip Hop feud of the 1990s after moving to California. Tupac read profusely and studied great thinkers, such as Shakespeare, Machiavelli, and Marx. His notable albums such as *Me Against the World* (1995) and *All Eyez on Me* (1996) delivered biting social commentary on issues such as poverty, the prison industrial complex, teen pregnancy, HIV/AIDS, economic policies, and police brutality. He is cited in the Guinness Book of World Records as having sold the most Hip Hop albums of all time (Dyson, 2001). And, his critically regarded book of poetry, aptly entitled, *The Rose that Grew from Concrete* (1999), which he wrote at nineteen years old, was also recorded as a spoken word CD of the same name (2000) by notable celebrities such as Danny Glover, Sonia Sanchez, Nikki Giovanni, and Quincy Jones reading his work.

TUPAC AND IDENTITY: ARTIST OR POLITICAL ACTIVIST?

Above all else, Tupac was an artist who represented a generation and a culture. Though he had legitimate activist roots, which along with lived experience as a working class man of color (Delgado & Stefanic, 2001) helped to garner his "authenticity" as an artist, he was neither an activist by definition nor an elected politician, yet his influence and adeptness in illuminating social issues was undisputed. Tupac was an artist, acclaimed actor, and a brilliant entertainer. He said it himself that he did not believe he was going to change the world, but he was sure his work and commentary (through his art) could "spark" social change. To this end, it is important to note that art holds an important place in any educational context because of its ability to critique existing social conditions (Felshin, 1995). A debate between scholars Michael Eric Dyson (2001) and Augusto Boal (Boal & McBride, 1979) might illuminate this tension over whether or not all art is political. Dyson (2001) asserts that Hip Hop may function in a political context but is not required to do so:

> ...its critics often fail to acknowledge that Hip Hop is neither sociological commentary nor political criticism, though it may certainly function in those modes through its artists' lyrics. Hip Hop is still fundamentally an art form that traffics in hyperbole, parody, kitsch, dramatic license, double entendres, signification and artistic merit. (p. xxi)

Dyson's assessment is accurate in the sense that Hip Hop is an art form, albeit not just rap music as he implied with the narrow definition of "lyrics," as the one way that Hip Hop artists can express themselves. They can also design clothes, create marketing campaigns, make films, and utilize drama, dance, and photography to represent themselves and their social commentary (Parker, 2003). However, he is right that it would still only be artistic rendition, not necessarily a social movement.

Hip Hop began as the voice of the underclass, the voice of marginalized people; it was about struggle, activism in the community, storytelling, and about having fun to relieve the stress of increasingly depressing social conditions. Hip Hop today remains fundamentally an art form that in and of itself is not necessarily always liberatory, nor is it entirely political or sociological commentary (Perry, 2004), though it can certainly be those things depending on which artists are being utilized. However it is intrinsically artistic and creative in its presentation of perspective. Dyson (2007) writes,

> By denying its musical and artistic merit, Hip Hop's critics get to have it both ways: they can deny the legitimate artistic standing of rap while seizing on its pervasive influence as an art form to prove what a terrible effect it has on youth. (p. xvii)

The contested nature of Hip Hop culture is clearly racialized, in that the personal "authenticity" of most (white) actors, popular music artists, or other artists is rarely questioned (Ogbar, 2007). Hip Hop artists are condemned for discussing "real" issues, whether or not they have actually experienced them (criminal, thug stereotype) or borne witness to someone else experiencing them (not criminal or "real" enough), despite the fact that (in either case) they are using their art to describe a phenomenon or situation. Meaning, a white artist can play a character that has a drug addiction or is a prostitute, but the expectation is never that they have actually experienced this phenomenon. In fact their ability to portray, write about, or otherwise chronicle someone else's experience authentically is often deemed worthy of accolades. However, many Hip Hop artists are critiqued if it is revealed that their street credibility is actually imaginative or representative commentary. Because Hip Hop as a cultural product is primarily created by urban youth of color, in a racist and classist system, it is difficult to imagine that the critics of Hip Hop, presenting their opinions through mainstream and conservative media (Rose, 2008), are able to understand Hip Hop as art in an equitable and affirming way. This is in many ways, perhaps, why "Dear Mama" was seen as so groundbreaking, because it was told in first person, verified narrative, so the authenticity of the artist, in this case Tupac Shakur, was not questioned. Could Drake or other artists have written a similar song, and would it have made it into the Library of Congress as bearing witness to cultural phenomena?

THE LASTING IMPRINT OF "DEAR MAMA"

From what I recall, 1995 was sort of a sappy and sentimental year for pop music, Boyz II Men and Mariah Carey broke all sorts of Billboard records with their bittersweet eulogy-style song, "One Sweet Day," and Bone Thugs-n-Harmony released their memorial album, *E. 1999 Eternal,* for N.W.A. member, Easy E. But overall, Hip Hop albums in 1995 were fairly masculine, with successful albums by commercially and critically acclaimed artists such as Raekwon, Mobb Deep, Pharcyde, and a return from KRS-One topping the charts. This is why, at least in part, Tupac's third album, *Me Against the World,* had such a reverberating impact. It was the first album to premiere at #1 on the Billboard rap charts from an artist who was incarcerated at the time of release, and it was a mixture of deep self-reflection and uncanny self-awareness, as well as straight up Hip Hop banter and prowess. It is likely that "Dear Mama," as the first single, went straight to #1 because it struck a chord with so many people due to the universality of under appreciating what parents go through in order to provide for their children, especially single parents in poor and working class environments. 2Pac's lyrics are poetic and poignant, and unfortunately still very timely:

> You always was committed
> A poor single mother on welfare, tell me how ya did it
> There's no way I can pay you back
> But the plan is to show you that I understand
> You are appreciated.
> (Shakur, 1995)

"Dear Mama" is rightfully deemed one of the greatest Hip Hop songs of all time, and it earned a place in the Library of Congress in 2010 because of its cultural significance, chronicling societal conditions in a first person narrative in real time from an "authentic" voice. This notable distinction means that by the National Recording Preservation Board's standards, "Dear Mama" has been deemed "culturally, historically, or aesthetically significant" and will join an elite group of only approximately 300 songs that have been inducted into the National Recording Registry. "The song displays further evidence of Hip Hop as a musically sophisticated and varied genre that can artfully encompass a wide variety of themes and musical influences" (Library of Congress, 2010).

"Dear Mama" has also been listed as one of the Top 100 Rap Songs in the world, by About.com (Adaso, 2013). It is considered by many to be 2Pac's most compelling and emotive song, is routinely cited by critics and artists alike as a Hip Hop gold standard, and is included in a book called *1001 Songs You Must Hear Before You Die: And 10,001 You Must Download* (Dimery, 2010). Because Tupac was incarcerated when "Dear Mama" was released, the video had to be shot without him. There are many shots of Afeni in the video, realistically portraying a mother reminiscing over her son's choices, and simultaneously celebrating his successes. An actor had to be brought in to portray Tupac in the scenes where he was featured.

> Dear Mama
> Place no one above ya, sweet lady
> You are appreciated
> Don't cha know we love ya?
> (Shakur, 1995)

In the years since Tupac's death, Afeni has honored his legacy in numerous ways. She founded the Georgia-based TupacAmaruShakurFoundation (TASF) in 1997 with the money made from Tupac's posthumous albums. TASF hosts a performing arts space for youth as well as community theater productions, a six-acre peace garden, and substantial art programs for young people, including a summer camp focusing on building self-esteem and confidence. In fact, at the recent Coachella performance, where the now infamous 2Pac hologram "performed," Dr. Dre reportedly donated over $100,000 to TASF in honor of Afeni's work and in order to use 2Pac's image. AmaruEntertainment, the primary business umbrella for all of Tupac's unreleased material, has produced posthumous albums and a well-known documentary about the artist entitled *Tupac: Resurrection* (Lazin, 2003). Afeni has also since launched a fashion clothing line, MakaveliBranded, and artists such as DJ Quik, Ludacris, BoneThugs-n-Harmony, and Chingy have appeared in marketing materials for the clothing line (http://hiphopenquirer.com/afeni-shakur-to-debut-makaveli-clothing-line/). Portions of proceeds from both companies go to TASF (Guy, 2004). And Clark Atlanta University's Robert W. Woodruff Library, supported through the Atlanta University Center, holds the largest and most complete Tupac Amaru Shakur collection of archived materials available to date.

DEAR MAMA: TODAY, TOMORROW AND YESTERDAY

In fall 2010, I was co-teaching a class at New York University, called "Lyrics on Lockdown," a social justice course where NYU students create arts-based workshops and go to the high school at Riker's Island to work with the young men who are incarcerated there. One of the groups chose to do a lesson analyzing Hip Hop song lyrics and then have the young men write letters to a loved one. The NYU students chose "Dear Mama" for a variety of reasons. This was somewhat of a surprise to me given the fact that in 1995 when the song debuted, most of them were in kindergarten, and the Riker's students were likely not even born yet. However, as the song started to play, it was clear to me that everyone knew the song; every person in the room—including the corrections officers—started singing along. And by the time the song ended, half the room was in tears; the NYU students and the Riker's students had very powerful reactions to the song, as it clearly resonated on many levels. In their letters, the Riker's students reflected on the guilt and sadness they were holding on to, for hurting their mothers by making decisions that took them away from their families. It was chilling to see that fifteen years later, "Dear Mama" was just as timely as ever, and for this reason, and so many more, it will forever remain a testimony in the complex tapestry of who and what Hip Hop is really about. And the power of art, to spark the minds of those who might change the world, is passed down to another generation.

REFERENCES

Adaso, H. (August 20, 2013). *Top 10 rap songs.* Retrieved July 27, 2012 from http://rap.about.com/od/top10songs/ss/Top100RapSongs.htm

Boal, A., & McBride, C. A. (1979). *Theatre of the oppressed.* New York, NY: Theatre Communications Group and Urizen Books.

Delgado, R., & Stefanic, J. (2001). *Critical race theory.* New York, NY: New York University Press.

Dimery, R. (2010). *1001 Songs you must hear before you die: And 10,001 you must download.* New York, NY: Universe Publishing. List retrieved, July 25, 2012 from http://www.listology.com/thisisentertainment/list/1001-songs-you-must-hear-you-die

Dyson, M. E. (2001). *Holler if you hear me: Searching for Tupac Shakur.* New York, NY: Basic Civitas Books.

Dyson, M. E. (2007). *Know what I mean? Reflections on hip-hop.* New York, NY: Basic Civitas Books.

Felshin, N. (1995). *But is it art?: The spirit of art as activism.* Castro Valley, CA: Bay Area Press.

Guy, J. (2004). *Afeni Shakur: Evolution of a revolutionary.* New York, NY: Atria Books.

Lazin, L. (Director). (2010). *Tupac: Resurrection* [Documentary]. United States: Amaru Entertainment Inc.

Library of Congress. (2010). *The sounds of fighting men, howlin' wolf and comedy icon among 25 named to the National Recording Registry.* Retrieved July 30, 2012 from http://www.loc.gov/today/pr/2010/10-116.html

Ogbar, O. G. (2007). *Hip-hop revolution: The culture and politics of rap.* Lawrence, KS: University Press of Kansas.

Parker, K. (2003). *Ruminations.* Brooklyn, NY: Welcome Rain Publishers.

Perry, I. (2004). *Prophets of the hood: Politics & poetics of hip-hop.* Durham, NC: Duke University Press.

Rose, T. (2008). *Hip-hop wars: What we talk about when we talk about hip-hop—and why it matters.* New York, NY: Basic Books.

Shakur, T. (1995). Dear mama. [Recorded by 2Pac]. On *Me against the world* [CD]. Santa Monica, CA: Interscope Records.

XXL magazine. Retrieved July 27, 2012 from http://www.xxlmag.com/news/latest-headlines/2010/06/tupacs-dear-mama-inducted-into-library-of-congress-registry

CHAPTER 14

"STRAIGHT EDGE" BY MINOR THREAT

Ross Haenfler

FROM PUNK ROCK TO STRAIGHT EDGE—ORIGINS, CONTEXT, AND INITIAL SIGNIFICANCE OF "STRAIGHT EDGE"

No one could have predicted that Minor Threat's 46-second song, published in 1981, would spawn a worldwide movement of clean-living youth that still resonates over thirty years later. In fact, the idea that *not* smoking, drinking, doing drugs, and having casual sex would appeal to youth must have seemed preposterous following the hedonistic hippie and disco scenes of the 1960s and 1970s. The counterculture encouraged experimentation of all kinds, and bands such as the Velvet Underground made even heroin seem at once dangerous and sexy. Yet this song, born amidst a hardcore revolution, continues to inspire tens of thousands of people across the world, despite little promotion and almost no airplay. "Straight edge" (MacKaye, 1981) shows the powerful potential of music beyond moving people to dance to actually *moving* people to action.

Written in the context of a punk rock culture often saturated with drugs, the song reflected some punks' unease with the self-destructive "no-future" attitude prevalent in the scene at the time. Minor Threat's Ian MacKaye,

Rebel Music, pages 131–139

Jeff Nelson, Brian Baker, and Lyle Preslar grew up in the Washington, D.C. punk scene. They loved the countercultural spirit, the passionate music, the do-it-yourself (DIY) ethic, and the question-everything mentality of punk but did not appreciate the scene's more nihilistic tendencies. In part, "Straight Edge" was a reaction to hard drug use that made the 1977 punks' glue-sniffing seem quaint. In 1972 New York Dolls drummer Billy Murcia, drowned in the course of a drug overdose, began what would become a string of drug-related deaths of musicians connected to punk rock. The Sex Pistol's Sid Vicious died of a heroin overdose in 1979, and the Germs' Darby Crash followed suit a year later in an OD/suicide. Keith Morris of seminal hardcore band Black Flag and Mike Ness of Social Distortion were among many punk rockers who experimented with heroin and other drugs. While punk purported to be something different from the standard folk and stadium rock fare, in the drug department it offered up more of the same. Janis Joplin, Jimi Hendrix, and Jim Morrison were only a few of the rising rock stars to have their lives cut short by drugs not long before punk's debut. Yet despite their disdain of hippies and mainstream pop music, punks largely supplanted sex, drugs, and rock and roll with sex, drugs, and *punk* rock and roll. In a sense, straight edge became a counterculture within a counterculture, a way for punks to truly distinguish themselves. After all, if drinking and drug use are the norm, then *not* using becomes the new rebellion, the punkest way to be punk.

In "Straight Edge," Ian MacKaye did not intend to generate a drug-free philosophy that would resonate with so many people over the course of thirty years; he intended, primarily, to challenge fellow punks and others in his local context that didn't accept his abstinence (Azerrad, 2001). He felt as if everyone in his high school was drinking and smoking pot, making *him* the outsider, and in that regard his fellow punks were no better. The young MacKaye explained in the 1984 documentary *Another State of Mind*, "When I became a punk my main fight was against the people that were around me, the kids, my friends that I saw and said 'God, I don't want to be like these people.' I didn't feel like I fit in at all with them" (Small & Stuart, 1984). Still, what began as a song gradually became a movement as youth across the U.S. adopted the straight edge lifestyle and identity, and bands such as Reno's 7 Seconds, Boston's SSD, and Los Angeles' Uniform Choice began promoting clean living in their lyrics. Eventually, youth began forming *straight edge bands* (e.g., Youth of Today) in which all members foreswore drugs and alcohol and took an active stance against intoxication. Since its beginnings in the 1980s, youth around the world, from Sweden to Argentina and South Africa to Indonesia, have taken up the straight edge identity. While "Straight Edge" provided the name and the general spirit of the growing movement, another Minor Threat song, 1983's "Out of Step," furnished its foundation: "(I) Don't Smoke, I don't drink, I don't fuck, At least I can fucking think" (MacKaye, 1983). Straight edgers abstain, completely, from drinking alcohol, using tobacco products, taking recreational drugs, and, in many cases, pursuing "casual" sex. They frame their choice as a lifetime commitment and most suggest that one sip of beer, one drag off a cigarette forfeits any claim to the identity. Most "straight edgers" have, at one time or another, displayed the movement's universal symbol, an X, scrawled in black magic marker on their hands or tattooed on their bodies. Straight edge clothing sports slogans such as "One Life Drug Free," "Poison Free," and "True 'Til Death," enabling straight edgers to literally wear their politics on their sleeves. While straight edge traces its roots to hardcore music, today you can find adherents in Hip Hop, metal, indie, and other scenes. Some dress like old-school punks, some like hardcore kids, some adopt emo, skater, and hipster fashions, and others blend in with their more mainstream peers.

In the remainder of the chapter, I discuss how "Straight Edge" and the movement it inspired challenge drug and alcohol culture, how such resistance is symbolic of a larger cultural resistance, and how straight edge exemplifies a lifestyle movement encouraging adherents to take action in their daily lives.

RESISTING DRUG CULTURE... AND MORE

First and foremost, straight edge, both the song and the movement, challenge the taken-for-granted role of intoxicating substances in many cultures. Alcohol is part of virtually every social event, from dinner parties and barbecues to baseball games and weddings. We learn that alcohol is useful for celebrating and mourning, getting to know people and getting laid. This is particularly true for youth, perhaps especially on college campuses. While not all college students drink, and many drink responsibly, getting wasted has long been woven into the fabric of college life, so much so that many colleges and universities consider "binge drinking" one of the most significant problems on campus. In such contexts, drinking becomes just "what you do," without a lot of thought put into why.

For generations of young people, drugs were subversive, a symbolic and sensual separation from their elders' staid, conformist, even oppressive ideas. The Beats and the hippies believed certain drugs could expand consciousness, providing insights and experiences otherwise unreachable. So when MacKaye sings "I've got better things to do/Than sit around and fuck my head/Hang out with the living dead" (MacKaye, 1981), he is reframing intoxication as a stupid waste of time, something that *fucks* you up rather than *lifts* you up. The "living dead" are *less* in tune with the world, zombies under a spell. Given the pressure many young people feel to drink, smoke, or use drugs to fit in, to be "cool," in challenging substance use "Straight Edge" upends one of the central tenets of youth, suggesting the popularity game itself is laughable. This basic idea—that doing something just because everyone else is doing it is absurd—underlies much of straight edge politics.

While straight edgers criticize the personal costs of drug, tobacco, and alcohol abuse, they also typically allow that individual users are caught in a larger, exploitative system. Alcohol and tobacco companies spend big money to hook young people on their products. For decades, the cigarette industry suppressed or denied smoking's negative health effects. They designed Joe Camel, the Marlboro Man, and more recently, flavored cigarettes to lure in younger smokers, hoping they get addicted young and become lifetime customers. Ruling in favor of the Justice Department's RICO suit against tobacco companies, U.S. District Court Judge Gladys Kessler described how they actively sought younger people as "replacement smokers" to fill in for those who quit or died off. Kessler wrote, "[the] Defendants have marketed and sold their lethal product with zeal, with deception, with a single-minded focus on their financial success, and without regard for the human tragedy or social costs that success exacted" (United States of America vs. Philip Morris USA, Inc. 2006). While the straight edge movement encourages individuals to take personal responsibility for their own sobriety, many adherents also acknowledge the deck is stacked against young people, that alcohol and drug culture is bigger than individual choices.

Additionally, while "Straight Edge" focuses on drug use, even from its inception the straight edge movement, like punk, encouraged critical thinking on a broader scale. Refusing drugs was symbolic, for many, of a greater resistance to "conventional" society and youth culture (Haenfler, 2004a). As MacKaye described seeing the Cramps play at his first punk rock show,

> Every given was really challenged at this gig. At that moment I realized here was a community that was politically confrontational, that was theologically confrontational, that was artistically confrontational, that was sexually confrontational, physically confrontational, musically confrontational. (Azzerad, 2001, p. 122)

Gradually, many straight edgers, like their punk brethren, molded and refined their general oppositional consciousness into opposing violence, sexism, corporate power, environmental destruction, and so on. For example, many straight edge kids adopt vegetarian or vegan lifestyles, viewing their personal choices as a collective challenge to animal cruelty. They report that being drug-free gives them a "clear mind" with which to better see society's illusions, oppressions, and injustices (Haenfler, 2006). A clear mind, they claim, increases their ability to control their circumstances and make countercultural choices.

PURSUING A CLEAR MIND—POP CULTURE, DRUGS, ALCOHOL AND CULTURAL HEGEMONY

"Straight Edge" bluntly suggests that sobriety (i.e., being straight) provides one an edge, an advantage over everyone else: "I've got the straight edge." MacKaye explained, "It's not saying I'm better. It's saying I got my head straight, I've got my shit together, and that's why I've got the advantage on you" (Small & Stuart, 1984). Contrary to the hippies, straight edgers pursue self-actualization via a *clear* mind rather than mind-altering substances. The lines "Always gonna keep in touch/Never want to use a crutch" suggest that people use drugs and alcohol as escapist tools to avoid problems and, perhaps, as a *shortcut* to enlightenment. Clean living, straight edgers argue, requires being in touch with one's emotions, facing one's problems head on. As MacKaye says, "I always knew life was precious and that I wanted to be present for every moment" (Small & Stuart, 1984). But the spirit of straight edge, as MacKaye intimates, was about more than pot, booze, and sex. It was about being an individual in a society that manufactures conformity, a society drunk not only on liquor but also *Survivor* and *Spongebob Squarepants*, professional wrestling and porn.

The fast, abrasive music exemplified by "Straight Edge," the manic delivery, and the frenetic dancing at shows issued a sonic and embodied challenge to pop musical conventions. As a *hardcore* song, "Straight Edge" offered, like the larger punk scene, a DIY alternative to the stadium rock fare popular at the time. But what does such a challenge ultimately accomplish? Academics and subculturists alike have long debated the role of pop culture in our lives—is it harmless entertainment, a simple escape from our workaday lives? Or does it lull us into passivity, numbing us to social injustices while turning us into insatiable consumers? Sociologists and philosophers Theodor Adorno and Max Horkheimer (1944) theorized a *culture industry* that mass produces relatively standardized cultural goods—TV shows, movies, magazines, music—for mass consumption, in a sense stupefying people and making them easier to manipulate. Content after a long work day to settle in for a beer and an episode of *Law and Order*, the average person then a) fails to see the larger oppressive systems in which she/he exists and participates; b) falls prey to misinformation, stereotypes, consumerism, and propaganda; or c) pays attention to the world's problems but, presented with few solutions or ways to get involved, feels powerless to do anything about them and so disengages. Addicted, in a way, not only to soda and potato chips but also to mental junk food, too many of us take capitalism for granted and find politics a bore, which is exactly what those with power and privilege count on, exercising a form of soft power in which people argue the merits of the latest reality TV show contestants in lieu of demanding fairness and justice. For critical theorists such as Adorno and Horkheimer, pop music, and pop culture in general, were just another means of pacifying the masses; even education, politics, and religion fall victim to the entertainment imperative as open political discourse gives way to "amusing ourselves to death" (Postman, 2005). Alcohol, tobacco, and drugs are marketed as youth "rebellion," despite being integral to most mainstream social gatherings. Following this logic, alcohol might be just another component of *mass culture*, part of a homogenized set of experiences promoted via the media for the sake of profiting from the highest number of consumers. If *American Idol* and *America's Next Top Model* can grip the nation's consciousness, imagine what mind-altering substances can do? While later scholarship challenges the portrayal of people as passive media consumers and uncritical cultural dopes (e.g., Jenkins, 1992, 2006), straight edge offers an actionable statement of defiance to perceived cultural hegemony.

But does a clear mind *really* give adherents an edge? Is straight edgers' cultural challenge significant and meaningful, or is straight edge just another social scene that reproduces the same tired social patterns in an X'd up form? Clearly straight edgers display a certain degree of arrogance in thinking a clear mind automatically gives one an edge over others, and it's not as if people who smoke and drink are automatically politically disengaged. Scholars of youth culture have long debated the significance of *youth resistance*. British researchers associated with the Centre for Contemporary Cultural Studies (also known as the Birmingham School) viewed youth subcultures such as skinheads and punks as working class youth engaged in symbolic resistance against their subordinate social position (e.g., Hebdige, 1979; Hall & Jefferson, 1976). Such youth resisted upper class *hegemony*, the monopoly on privilege and power, via their spectacular styles and rituals. However, according to the Birmingham School, their resistance was ultimately illusory, resolving none of the underlying inequalities and injustices. A spiky leather jacket, bondage gear, and a Mohawk may startle conventional onlookers, and even upend fashion conventions, they but do little to reduce social inequality. (In fact, being a punk may *reinforce* one's subordinate position.) Likewise, not drinking and using may be personally beneficial, but straight edge's emphasis on self-control and abstinence reflects values found in mainstream religious circles.

From the outset, some punks did not take kindly to straight edgers, finding them boring and conservative at best, arrogant and self-righteous at worst (O'Hara, 2001). "Bent edge" groups heckled Minor Threat at shows. After all, the very idea of a set of *rules* ran counter punk's "no rules!" ethos, though MacKaye insisted in "Out of Step" that "this is no set of rules," suggesting that he was merely screaming about his personal choices in response to the flack he took for being straight. Still, while the overwhelming majority of adherents condemn violence, the judgmental, holier-than-thou straight edge "tough guy" became the most visible face of straight edge in some scenes, as well as in the mainstream media. A minority of straight edgers has enforced its credo with violence, forming straight edge "crews" and picking fights. Such hyper masculine behavior marginalizes women, painting a contradictory portrait of a supposedly anti-sexist, "positive" subculture (Haenfler, 2004b). Perhaps the counter-hegemonic potential of music scenes, and songs like "Straight Edge," is rather limited. How we judge the impact of music depends in part upon how we conceptualize social change.

STRAIGHT EDGE AS A LIFESTYLE MOVEMENT

What does "Straight Edge" teach us about pursuing social change? Popular images of social change tend towards the dramatic: *social movements*—such as civil rights—or *revolutions*—such as the Arab uprisings—accomplish "real" change, while subcultures related to music scenes are simply temporary playgrounds for adolescents. Straight edge challenges such assumptions in several ways, illustrating a different sort of politics, a politics focused less on activist organizations engaging in public protest against the government and more on informally connected individuals making (relatively) private, personal choices directed at culture norms. In this sense, straight edge is a *lifestyle movement*, a "loosely bound [collectivity] in which participants advocate lifestyle change as a primary means to social change" (Haenfler, Johnson, & Jones, 2012, p. 14). Voluntary simplicity, slow food, virginity pledge, locavore, and fair trade movements are other prominent examples. In the tradition of feminists, anarchists, environmentalists, and others, straight edge illustrates that the *personal is political*, breaking down the dichotomy between personal and social transformation. What distinguishes this sort of politics from simple lifestyle choices is its outward focus and the recognition that one's personal decisions, taken in concert with likeminded others, add up to a collective challenge. In other words, adopting a vegan lifestyle solely for personal health is different from understanding such a diet as a political act in defiance of corporate agribusiness and animal cruelty.

"Advertising" one's lifestyle politics, whether through evangelism or simply leading by example, opens up possibilities for others to take similar action. Many straight edgers, especially younger ones, openly display their affiliation, certainly to show their "subcultural capital," but also as a statement against alcohol and drug culture (Thornton, 1995; Haenfler, 2004a, 2006). They sew Xs on their school bags, paste stickers on their cars, wear them on their clothes, and tattoo Xs on their bodies (Atkinson, 2003; Wood, 2006). The very act of recording "Straight Edge" and making the song public demonstrates an intention to challenge social convention. Anyone, presumably, can abstain from drugs, tobacco, and alcohol; on some level, being drug-free is simply a lifestyle choice. However, the act of making that choice public, of leading by example, of creating possibilities for others, transforms straight edge from just another personal choice into a cultural challenge. Critics may charge straight edge kids with being "preachy"—and sometimes they are. But surely alcohol and tobacco ads, or "ladies night" and other promotions so common we take them for granted, constitute "preaching" on a much larger scale.

For some straight edgers, the identity's meaning begins and ends with abstinence. When straight edge resistance stops at exchanging bar culture for hardcore shows, then perhaps straight edge is little more than a social club (although carving out a cultural space for youth who don't drink, but also don't fit in, to feel accepted, be creative, and have fun is no trivial accomplishment). When people's efforts begin and end with tweaks to their diet and consumption, they may lose sight of the big picture and bask in self-satisfaction. However, as I have shown, many straight edgers connect their clean living commitment and identity to other issues, seeing such concerns as a logical progression from having a "clear mind." Some even join their edge identity to radical activism, feminism, anarchism, queer politics, anti-fascism, global democracy protests, and so on (see Kuhn, 2010). Many straight edgers have taken punk's DIY ethic and straight edge's clean living as a call to accomplish bigger goals, to live outside the box, to go against the grain, and to engage the world more fully. The point is that not all efforts at change take place in the streets or the halls of Congress. Lifestyle movements help shift the cultural discourse, can change dominant relationships, and encourage people to take action in their daily lives. They also serve as a bridge to more traditional political participation and protest politics. "Straight Edge" is about resisting dominant expectations and taking some measure of responsibility for creating alternatives—DIY applies not just to making music, but also to generating social change.

REFERENCES

Adorno, T., & Horkheimer, M. (1944). *Dialectic of enlightenment.* Palo Alto, CA: Stanford University Press.

Atkinson, M. 2003. The civilizing of resistance: Straightedge tattooing. *Deviant Behavior, 24,* 197–220.

Azzerad, M. 2001. *Our band could be your life: Scenes from the American indie underground 1981–1991.* New York, NY: Little, Brown and Company.

Haenfler, R. (2004a). Rethinking subcultural resistance: Core values of the straight edge movement. *Journal of Contemporary Ethnography, 33*(1), 406–436.

Haenfler, R. (2004b). Manhood in contradiction: The two faces of straight edge. *Men and Masculinities, 7,* 77–99.

Haenfler, R. (2006). *Straight edge: Clean-living youth, hardcore punk, and social change.* New Brunswick, NJ: Rutgers University Press.

Haenfler, R., Johnson, B., & Jones, E. (2012). Lifestyle movements: Exploring the intersection of lifestyle and social movements. *Social Movement Studies, 11*(1), 1–20.

Hall, S., & Jefferson, T. (Eds.). (1976). *Resistance through rituals: Youth subcultures in post-war Britain.* London, England: Unwin Hyman.

Hebdige, D. (1979). *Subculture: The meaning of style.* London: Methuen.

Jenkins, H. (1992). *Textual poachers: Television fans and participatory culture.* New York, NY: Routledge.

Jenkins, H. (2006). *Fans, bloggers, and gamers: Exploring participatory culture.* New York, NY: New York University Press.

Kuhn, G. (2010). *Sober living for the revolution: Hardcore punk, straight edge, and radical politics.* Oakland, CA: PM Press.

MacKaye, I. (1981). Straightedge [Recorded by Minor Threat]. On *Minor Threat* [7" Vinyl]. Washington, DC: Dischord.

MacKaye, I. (1983). Out of Step [Recorded by Minor Threat]. On *Out of Step* [7" Vinyl]. Washington, DC: Dischord.

O'Hara, C. (2001). *The philosophy of punk: More than noise.* Oakland, CA: AK Press.

Postman, N. (2005). *Amusing ourselves to death: Public discourse in the age of show business.* New York, NY: Penguin Books.

Small, A., & Stuart, P. (Writers/Directors). (1984). *Another state of mind* [Documentary]. United States: Coastline Films.

Thornton, S. (1995). *Club cultures: Music, media and subcultural capital.* Middletown, CT: Wesleyan University Press.

United States of America, et. al. vs. Phillip Morris USA, Inc. et. al. Civil Action No. 99-2496. United States District Court for the District of Columbia. Accessed online http://www.justice.gov/sites/default/files/civil/legacy/2014/09/11/amended%20opinion_0.pdf (November 4, 2014).

Wood, R. T. (2006). *Straightedge: Complexity and contradictions of a subculture.* Syracuse, NY: Syracuse University Press.

PART VIII

COMMUNITY

CHAPTER 15

"IT WAS A GOOD DAY" BY ICE CUBE

Emery Petchauer

Hip Hop is a lot of things, and often times it is autobiographical. When a graffiti writer paints a throw-up on a wall to represent her moniker, it is a visual inscription of self, the world's most succinct autobiography. When a b-girl creates and dances a set—with top rock, footwork, spin moves, and a freeze—it is a statement to all others in the cypher about who she is, what she represents. When a DJ, in the limited amount of time between records, selects a song to play, he is doing so based upon his personal experience with each song and a judgment about how it might move the crowd. And perhaps most explicitly, emcees speak autobiographically when they reflect upon and document the events in their lives in their rhymes.

In Ice Cube's "It Was a Good Day" (Jackson, 1992), a popular track from his 1992 album *The Predator*, Cube raps over a smooth loop from the Isley Brother's "Footsteps in the Dark," a haunting song from 1977 that centers on a lover questioning the faithfulness and dedication of his partner in their rocky relationship. Over this groove, Cube works according to this autobiographical aspect of Hip Hop as he documents in chronological order from sunup to sundown the mundane, enjoyable, and even fantastical events in what he proclaims is "a good day." In his excellent work on

Rebel Music, pages 143–148

bboying/bgirling (a form of Hip Hop dance), Joe Schloss (2009) unpacks how the pioneers of this dance form—as youth—took elements of their daily lives and infused them into the dance: competitiveness, boasting, sexuality, social status, play, popular films, and more. As there is coherence among the different expressions and elements of Hip Hop, the same is present in "It Was a Good Day." Cube's narrative touches on driving around in a tricked-out car, hanging out with friends, beating everyone at basketball and other games, being desired my multiple women, setting up and executing a sexual hook-up, drinking alcohol, and being wary of encounters with police and carjackers. In these ways, the track is like other elements of Hip Hop culture: the creator infuses his or her unique experience—some real, some exaggerated—into the form. Under the mantra of keeping it real, this stamp of individuality makes the narrative a more authentic product within the Hip Hop cypher.

The contents of "It Was a Good Day" also coincide with the "hyper local" qualities of Hip Hop culture. Murray Forman (2002) discusses this characteristic in his work on race and space in Hip Hop music. He argues that space is more of an idea (a social construct) in Hip Hop music than it is a real location. Certainly, locations such as South Central, the South Bronx, and South Philly are real places, but more importantly in Hip Hop culture, there are real and imagined ideas that people associate with these places. This is also true of more abstract places such as "the 'hood" or "the West Coast." According to these qualities, this means that artists such as Ice Cube highlight ideas, norms, images, items, practices, or artifacts that are associated with a specific place. Along these same lines, Jeff Chang (2005) describes this as a "hood-centric aesthetic" that was initiated by N.W.A.'s first album, *Straight Outta Compton*:

> After *Straight Outta Compton*, it really was all about where you were from. N.W.A. conflated myth and place, made the narratives root themselves on the corner of every 'hood. And now every 'hood could be Compton, everyone had a story to tell. (p. 321)

This hyper-local and 'hood-centric quality is present throughout Cube's narrative as he alludes to and references things associated with southern California, or South Central Los Angeles more specifically. These include pollution (smog), outdoor car culture (drop tops and jackers,), hydraulics and other car modifications (switches and three-wheel motion), dominos, the Los Angeles Lakers, the regional restaurant Fatburger, and the A.K. 47 firearm. Without a doubt, items such as these are not limited to Los Angeles. However, in music, film, and the popular imagination, these represent the *idea* of Los Angeles, particularly in the 1990s. If one examines the song as portrayed in the music video, these elements of L.A. become even clearer, especially through fashion. Ice Cube wears a black and grey flannel with a black bandana twisted up neatly around his head. These colors and wardrobe items are common in portrayals of L.A. in the 1990s, particularly in relation to gangs. Cube's colors, however, signal a neutral gang affiliation. The Bloods and Crips are also represented in the video by men wearing red and blue flannels and bandanas, respectively, attending a funeral of one of their members. These images of L.A., regardless of how real or imagined they are, root the narrative firmly in L.A. and thus give Cube's account of this good day authenticity by Hip Hop's standards.

THE PRESENCE OF DEATH

While the above items from Cube's good day are relatively benign, he also references something else that was prevalent in Los Angeles in the 1990s and even today for many Black and Brown males: death. In each verse of the song, Cube makes clear that lingering between the everyday pleasures of young adult good days is the possibility of death. He contemplates before leaving home, "Will I live another 24?" He is relieved that there are no carjackers attempting to steal his custom car as he stops at a red light (a crime featured in 1990s movies such *Menace II Society*). In seeing police drive past, he recalls how they tried to shoot him the previous day. As he drives home at the end of the day, he notes that there's "No helicopter looking for a murder."

While these possibilities of death are interwoven with the daily events in his narrative, others are juxtaposed and somewhat startling interjections. One of these instances comes in the last four bars of the second verse as Cube recounts a long list of successes competing against his friends.

> I picked up the cash flow
> Then we played bones, and I'm yellin' "domino"
> Plus nobody I know got killed in South Central L.A.
> Today was a good day.
> (Jackson, 1992)

The placement of Cube's recognition that nobody he knew got killed is sudden but also peculiar. It neither fits nor flows after he recounts serving his friends at a dice game of craps and then dominos. The peculiar placement makes it seem as if regardless of those prior good fortunes, a lack of death among his acquaintances is an essential quality of a good day. An identical interjection in the same line location comes in the third verse as Cube drives home to conclude his day.

Drunk as hell but no throwin' up
Halfway home and my pager still blowin' up
Today I didn't even have to use my A.K.
I gotta say it was a good day.
(Jackson, 1992)

Once again, the possibility and absence of violence interrupts the list of occurrences that make up a good day. As in the end of verse two, there is an assumption that he regularly does have to use his assault rifle and a bit of surprise that it was not necessary on this day.

POLITICS AS (UN)USUAL

Listening to "It Was a Good Day," one might get the sense that Cube rapped over smooth grooves about PG-13 events in the lives of young males throughout this career. This sense would fit with most of Cube's films since the 2002 *Barbershop* as well as his family-friendly shows such as *Are We There Yet?* It would be easy to draw a direct line from "It Was a Good Day" to Cube's current work in film and television, but this line would be entirely false.

In the 1990s, Cube was one of the lead figures in a cadre of Hip Hop artists who were lyrically terrorizing mainstream white America. His career began in the late 1980s as part of N.W.A—a group that did not create the genre known as "gangsta rap" but certainly thrust it and its real and mythic narratives of street life into mainstream America. After leaving the group for his solo career and coming into the tutelage of the Nation of Islam and the larger body of Black liberation thought, Cube became an even bigger agitator to the established order when his music no longer just chronicled street life but applied a strong (albeit, deeply flawed) political lens to it. If Cube was narrating aspects of street life before, now he was targeting the groups, individuals, and government institutions who were responsible for the societal inequalities that made street life possible.

His first solo album, the 1990 *Amerikkka's Most Wanted,* illustrates this in a few ways. Shaped by the brilliant production team the Bomb Squad, the album's title flipped the title of a popular television show of that era, *America's Most Wanted.* Beginning in 1988 and running for 23 years, the show featured profiles of real criminals to aid in their arrest and conviction. Cube signifies on—or flips the meaning of—the show in the title of his album, thus making himself one of America's Most Wanted. Importantly, Cube (and to be fair, the team of people who helped craft the album) add a reference to the Ku Klux Klan (i.e., KKK) *inside* of the word "America" in the title of this album to make the racist white supremacy group and the country of America inseparable. That is, in this act of signifying, America is made up of the KKK. This critique of America—as well as hateful attacks on Jewish folks, gay folks, woman, Asians, and others—were not limited to album titles. The contents of *Amerikka's Most Wanted* and its provocative and inflammatory follow up, *Death Certificate,* were also attacks that received national attention, protest, and calls for boycotts.

The album context of "It Was a Good Day" also illustrates this quality of Cube's career. In *The Predator,* the track is sandwiched between the album's title cut and "We Had to Tear This Mothafucka Up." Both of these tracks directly address the L.A. uprising, protest, and riots that responded to the acquittal of four Los Angeles Police Department officers after the now-infamous Rodney King beating that took place prior to the album's release. Naming names, Cube calls out the officers in "The Predator," describes graphic violence against them, and threatens other groups as well. On the other side of "It Was a Good Day," the lyrical riot continues in "We Had to Tear This Mothafucka Up." With the title alluding to the necessity of looting and rioting, the track starts with samples of actual news commentary during the uprising. Compared sonically to "It Was a Good Day," the track (produced by DJ Muggs) is full of musical samples that create a dense collage of sound. Like the music of Public Enemy and Cube's earlier albums produced by the Bomb Squad, this sonic quality matches the chaotic and frantic content of the lyrics. Against this background is Cube's continued assault against the officers, judge, and jury of the trial—not to mention the President of the whole damn country. Seen in this context, "It Was a Good Day" does not represent the overall flavor of the album nor of Cube's early catalogue. It is simply a break from the regularly-scheduled, sonically-dense, and politically-aggressive program that was much of Ice Cube's music in the 1990s.

Despite the fact that "It Was a Good Day" is very much an outlier, it is the most well-known song from this album and of Cube's career to the general public. This should not be a surprise. In this era of the music industry before digital music and widespread social media like music blogs, mainstream radio play was more necessary for an artist to be successful. Consequently, record companies regularly released non-offensive music and catchy songs from albums (i.e., singles) to be played on the radio and generate interest in the entire album, even though some songs from the album would never be played on the radio. "It Was a Good Day" indeed attracted much attention to *The Predator,* and it was *not* a good day for some unsuspecting listeners when they listened to the whole album.

ALL'S WELL THAT ENDS WELL

There is a clear irony that Ice Cube was once seen as one of the most threatening rap artists of the 1990s but today is known as a successful actor, director, and producer of mainstream and unoffending entertainment. In fact, many people who know Cube only through his post-2000 movies and shows may be unaware of his larger body of musical work touched on in this chapter. Today, he is far from the predator he might have been in the 1990s. This trajectory—from rapper to mainstream entertainer—is not only embodied by Cube. Many actors such as Will Smith, Common, LL Cool J, Queen Latifah, and others also started out as rappers. In a sense, the skill set it takes to emcee can translate to other arts such as acting. With these artists, however, their growth into acting is not saturated in the irony of Cube's growth. This irony could be said of Snoop Dogg and Ice T, who were also seen by mainstream white America as threats to so-called "family values" but now probably embody those values more than threaten them.

Luther Campbell (known as Luke of 2 Live Crew) also fits this irony. Once at the center of a 1990 landmark obscenity trial and controversy because of his sexually explicit music and performances, he is now known more for his community youth work around Miami and coaching high school football. From today's vantage point, some of the rap artists who caused the most alarm became perfectly acceptable contributors to entertainment and society. As the saying goes, all's well that ends well. One must ask though if the kind of critique that Cube and others gave to America was not also a type of contribution to society. While certainly not without flaw, his music helped show a wide cross-section of America a vision of society of which they were unaware. Cube helped make them aware, even if it was against their will.

REFERENCES

Chang, J. (2005). *Can't stop, won't stop: A history of the hip-hop generation.* New York, NY: Basic Books.

Forman, M. (2002). *The 'hood comes first: Race, space, and place in rap and hip-hop.* Middleton, CT: Wesleyan University Press.

Jackson, O. (1992). It was a good day [Recorded by Ice Cube]. On *The predator* [CD]. Los Angeles, CA: Priority Records.

Schloss, J. (2009). *Foundation: B-boys, b-girls, and hip-hop culture in New York.* Oxford, UK: Oxford University Press.

CHAPTER 16

"WELCOME TO PARADISE" BY GREEN DAY

Michael Loadenthal

WARMINSTER, PENNSYLVANIA: 1994

"Welcome to Paradise" always makes me smile when I hold it up to the narrative that is the memory of my life. I had first heard it in 1994, while in the fifth grade, after buying the cassette at The Wall. When I heard it as a kid, I always imagined the subject of the song as Tom Hank's *Big* character, Josh Baskin, who cries himself to sleep in the first night of his big city apartment. I imagined a boy, scared, hearing gunshots outside his window overlooking "cracked streets" and "broken homes." I always imagined an *othered* subject, but reflecting back on the track as an adult, I saw myself.

On the first of February, 1994, Reprise Records released *Dookie*, Green Day's third studio album. Anyone alive and aware at the time will remember. The album went on to reach number two on the U.S. Billboard charts, place on sales charts in six other countries, and a year later, won a Grammy for "best alternative music album." For many, this was when Green Day sold out, but for me, it was when they were born.

The album was less than forty minutes, with fourteen tracks packed in. As we all know, real punk gems weigh in at less than three minutes apiece, so the formula worked. The album had five singles. "Welcome to Paradise"

Rebel Music, pages 149–157

(Armstron, 1994) was one of them. Strangely, it wasn't even a new song for the band, as it had appeared on their1992 album *Kerplunk.* The lyrics are reportedly based on the band members' experience of moving out of their parents' homes and into an Oakland squat. Though the band's group house was occupied rent-free, and my less-than-stellar housing situations have always been rented, I can still relate. I moved out of my parent's house at eighteen and went straight to Washington, DC, a city with a violent crime and murder rate rivaling all other national locales.

When I moved to DC and into a group house with my fellow anarchist-vegan activists, we were society's vagabonds, just like the artists and musicians that occupied the Green Day's squat. The space that inspired Green Day's hit song—a particularly sketchy "crusty punk squat"—was in fact a West Oakland warehouse situated overtop a brothel. For Green Day it was a crash pad, but for me, when I moved to DC, my squat was my new home. The group/collective houses we helped to build in DC were modeled after our punk and do-it-yourself (DIY) ethics. We practiced and learned to live below our means—to get by outside of the 40-hour a week grind—in a city that rivals New York in price point.

In my time in DC, I lived all over and moved a lot. We kept a lease for a year and then hopped to the next new deal via the free market, direct-to-consumer buying power of Craigslist. On one of the few occasions when my mother made the trek to visit me in DC, and I took her around, all I could hear in my head was the famous refrain, "I want to take you through a wasteland I like to call my home." By the time I was able to act as a tour guide for the family, the "broken homes" and "cracked streets" *had* become my home.

In "Welcome to Paradise," the storyteller is heard recording a message on his mother's answering machine, reporting back since he'd left home. My mother and I did this via email and phone as well, and like the storyteller in the song, after a few months of report backs, any bit of hesitation and oddity became familiar, even a proud point of reference. In such a short time, the scary and new becomes the mundane and daily. That is one message of the song. The other message is one of gentrification—generations of white kids raised just outside city limits who, when given their first chance, rush back to the very urban centers their parents were so proud to have escaped. For my parents it was Reagan-era "white flight" that drove them into the suburbs, but for Generation X/Y it is something quite different.

I took lessons on racial relations and the modernity of neighborhood ghettos visiting and working in Philadelphia, but Warminster was my *home.* Warminster is a suburb, like so many others, four miles long and two miles wide, nestled in Bucks County, Pennsylvania's southeast corner. Because it is less than ten miles to Philly, many of us considered ourselves city folk.

My parents, aunts, uncles, grandparents, and great-grandparents lived and worked in Philadelphia. Exactly one year before I was born, my family moved from northeast Philadelphia to Warminster. I still came to the city to work with my parents and visit my grandparents, aunts, uncles, cousins, and friends. All of our family remained behind in the gritty city while my parents and sister moved twenty minutes northwest to suburbia.

Mine is not an uncommon story of punk for those of us entering our 30s, the youngins of the Boomers and the children of the 1980s. We grew up in a newly suburban punk America marked by shopping malls and skateboards. For our history as a family emigrating from the Old World, I was the first generation of suburbanites. Being a punk in the suburbs presents particularly unique problems with sublimely unique DIY solutions. We occupied space at strip malls and movie theaters when city corners were absent. We met each other at far off record exchanges and traveled in packs to see touring bands. Yes, the suburbs and punk are a natural pairing with a little do-it-yourself creativity correctly applied.

WASHINGTON, DC: 2002

In one sense, the suburbs are necessary for punk to flourish. While the emergence of 1980s hardcore allowed punk to be separated from its inner-city, working-class roots, the new suburban landscape it occupied was viewed through a smoke filled lens of contempt and loathing criticism. On the coastal cities where this shift began, some bands even embraced their suburban roots. As the suburbs shifted from mass residential—a place for commuter-type city folk to sleep—and slowly became home to the large-scale commercial sites of office parks, shopping malls, large retail chains and industrial facilities, the sleepy nature of places like Warminster began to take on new forms.

In journeying from Warminster to Washington, soon enough, the stories of my new surroundings became my own. In a rather rapid exchange and re-homing, *their* 'hood becomes *your* 'hood... or at least the place where you and your stuff reside. Soon enough, the scary of the city becomes the home you know, and quickly you forget the days that preceded your time there. In practice, I remained nomadic and un-homed. The "locals" seemed either disinterested or outright opposed to the idea of the creation of white-dominated, lefty enclaves, and who could blame them? It was likely they saw the writing on the wall. They knew what coffee shops and new condos would do to their rents. This is gentrification par excellence.

During this particular period of white *in*-flight to DC's upper northwest, the demographic change occurred so rapidly that even as an upwardly mobile, white-skinned service worker and university student, I was displaced from my newly gentrified surroundings in only five years (2002–2007). The area just got way too expensive, way too quickly. By 2012, the notable shift from families of Blacks and Latinos, to white folks under the age of 35 was palpable. The sociological observation was commonplace in the contemporary people's history of the city—the word on the street. It was a common topic of conversation, of news reporting, and of unavoidable commentary. Some say the apex of this was April 2012 when the *City Paper* displayed the cover story, "A Guide For The Responsible Gentrifier" (Schaffer, Schweitzer, Hilton, & Baca, 2012).

For my young life, my guide to cities had been my father, whose racism interpreted Philly's houseless population for me in our frequent interactions as corner-side food vendors. In DC, I moved east with my father's voice in my head. He always carried a concealed pistol while at work selling hotdogs and cheese-steaks from his sidewalk food cart. In our time together as boss and worker, I'd seen him pull his gun in action several times, including one incident involving a robbery and a second involving a cop. It was through these experiences that I interpreted DC's neighborhoods during my fractured tenures. It was through these experiences that I formulated my opposition to the racism and classism explained to me in my father's stories of the city.

Though my father was not a central player in my life during my 11-plus years in and out of DC, when I did relocate to "the 'hood" in 2002, my mother was worried. I was a 135 pound white boy with a Mohawk and a huge septum ring in an area of African American families, Howard University students, and Jamaican immigrants. Our trash can in the alley was an overflowing repository for hypodermic needles, and our front lawn, only feet from a busy intersection, was a place for drugs to be sold and for drunk people to be found asleep. "A gunshot rings out at the station," Billie Joe screams (Armstrong, 1994); yeah, in our neighborhood too. In fact, it was nearly a daily auditory event. My ten-minute walk down Georgia Avenue to the Metro was a site for racialized catcalls, so I made it a rule to wear a thick, black jacket and hoodie when walking home at night. If I kept my head down and my hands in my pockets, you couldn't tell I was white, or quite so slender.

"This sudden fear has left me trembling" (Armstrong, 1994); well yeah, being chased down a street while onlookers jeer can do that to a boy. On these nightly walks, it was not that I was trying to be something other than white; I was just trying to be unnoticed, to be part of the background. To be white was to draw attention, and to be noticed was to be the target of solicitation and harassment.

PHILADELPHIA, PENNSYLVANIA: 2007

When I moved back to Philly for a short stint in 2007, I lived near the heart of the historic town center where my dad and I sold hotdogs and cheese-steaks for so many years. Further to the south was Philadelphia's Italian area, centered around diagonally-positioned, competing cheese-steaks shops. In my youth, it was this area that exposed me to Philadelphia's Mafia. As a youngster I saw old Italian men taking receiving lines of visitors hidden in poorly lit dive bars. I was a frequent visitor to the mechanic's garage where machine guns were fired at a sound dampening drop cloth. One time I even sold ice cream cones to a group of neighborhood kids and was paid by "Skinny" Joey Merlinno, the presently incarcerated leader of Philadelphia's Scarfo crime family. He treated the whole block. When I saw how the Mafia-affiliated folks lived in nearly gated communities hidden within the city's center, I began to understand even more the idea of ethnic neighborhoods—modern day, self-imposed ghettos.

What I learned from being shown around Philly's neighborhoods—from the Italians to the Jews—is that neighborhoods change. My grandparents and parents grew up in what are now "Black areas" of Philly where white families do not reside. North and West Philadelphia were where my ancestors, the Cohen, Rice, Selevitz, and Loadenthal families, made homes when they came from Russia, Lithuania, and Poland near the turn of the 20th century. How it must have felt to be them. How did *their* song go? "Welcome to Paradise"? I'm not so sure for the new generation of immigrant Jewish-Americans. Like today's Washingtonian People of Color being pushed out of the city, my ancestors also knew firsthand the American experience of institutionalized racism and injustice. They were veterans of an Ellis Island that Germanicized *Low*enthal into *Load*enthal and Masha into Mary. A generation later, they would see their children's businesses destroyed in race riots. My white mother would teach Black kids at the public schools where she worked, and my white dad served Black customers at the newsstands and food cart. My father, the grandson of Eastern European Jews, often told customers he was *Italian* because it was more palatable than *Jew*.

All of this family capital generated in Philadelphia throughout the generations kept my sister and I in a largely white public school in a working class (read lower middle class) suburb. The town has some petrochemical manufacturers, machine parts factories, two EPA-rated superfund sites, and a train station at the end of the train line to center city Philadelphia. Warminster was and remains to be a working class city, though about 86% white according to a 2010 demographic survey.

My parents and grandparents were often in the ethnic minorities where they lived and worked in North, West, and South Philadelphia. Around the 1950s, many of the areas my family saw as "Jewish parts" became largely

Black. In the 2000s, the areas where I dwelled in DC were changed from Black and Latino families to white transient renters. Bikes became far more common, so the city built bike lanes. Soon came coffee shops, cafes, bars, restaurants, high-rise apartments, and swaths of new retail. Small, Salvadorian *pupuserias* started printing their menus in English and hiring bilingual workers. "Fish In the 'Hood," a local favorite, renamed itself "Fish In the *Neighbor*hood." In an article discussing the name change (Wax, 2012), the writer notes that the shift "seemingly captures a moment of transition in this city, where African Americans may be losing their majority status in the District for the first time in 50 years." Our neighborhood even got a vegan bakery with free Wi-Fi and fair-trade coffee. Intersections changed from empty lots, baseball fields, and a homeless shelter to "DC USA," a mega complex containing Best Buy, Target, Bed Bath & Beyond, Marshalls, Staples, and, of course, new condos.

We the new DCers claimed areas, group houses, and whole neighborhoods, though many of us were more transient than the Bedouins, and with far less claim to the land.

WHAT A LONG STRANGE TRIP IT'S BEEN

I can distinctly remember walking home from elementary school, knapsack on my back, Sony Walkman cassette player in my hand, rockin' to what was to me, a new punk sound. Green Day's *Dookie* would become my entry point to punk. Green Day to the Offspring, Offspring to the whole Epitaph catalog and their friends: NOFX, Pennywise, Agnostic Front, Dropkick Murphy's, Guttermouth, Rancid, Bad Religion, and so on. After that I discovered the "inner-city" punk scene concentrated in areas opened up to gentrification through a nearly siege-like push by the University of Pennsylvania. This led me to hardcore and crust. Locally it was Anti-Product, Kill the Man Who Questions, R.A.M.B.O. and Kid Dynamite. Later it was the politics of Aus-Rotten, Against All Authority, Choking Victim, Fifteen, Reagan Youth, Propagandhi, and even (very) early Anti-Flag—local anarcho-heroes of sorts. My love of punk preceded my love of Hip Hop, which I discovered around thirteen when a neighborhood friend and "wigger" was forced to give away his Wu-Tang and 2Pac CDs to me when his parents disapprovingly discovered them.

Like many anarchists of my time, I often pointed to punk as my entry point into this social war we call leftist politics. I was a veteran of the rec center, church, basement, and squat shows long before I ever made it to DC, and punk showed me many places I might not have otherwise seen, let alone called a place to hang out. When punk led me to anarchism and a neo-bourgeoning protest movement against capitalism gaining momentum in DC, I was truly thankful. "Welcome to [my] paradise" could have been the soundtrack to my cinematic montage of the five us of moving into that big row house. Like other college-aged white radicals, we entered a relatively nepotistic, insular community of veggie group houses. In one sense, not much has changed. I was (and am) vegan and was (and am) an advocate of total liberation through revolutionary change.

All generations (I think) like to look forward to the new kids as posers. We are outsiders that flood old communities, call them home, and then "defend" them against gentrification from the later folks following suit. We, the punks of the mid-to-late-1990s, were no different. I like to say that punk meant resistance back then at the end of the millennium, but by January 1, 2000, it had long since been dead. The Mohawks we all had, within ten years, became even less meaningful as they became a staple of hipster urbanites we all scorned.

By the time I was settled in DC, my musical sages had become Dilated Peoples, Talib, Ghostface, and NaS. All of a sudden, their messages became my own. Police, drugs, city streets, the hustle of making ends meet—all enveloped my days, and without the insular punk community, my interests and connections faded. Punk was my outside the house, concert, and basement show music, but inside my headphones it was 1990s Hip Hop all day.

"Punk," in whatever it means, helped to constitute my young self-identification with a subversive, oppositional subculture.

CINCINNATI, OHIO: 2013–PRESENT

When I agreed to write an article on "punk" and "identity," I hadn't imagined some meandering autobiography of my moves and tastes, but that is how I know to tell the story of Green Day's influence. It was situated in a certain time and place, and without these circumstances, I would not have the associations that I do. "Welcome to Paradise" became a reflection on delocalizing and gentrification when those themes became *my* reality. I didn't sit down to write about myself, but this is the task in examining identity construction—the stories that make "us" *us.* My father's stories of race and violence made me want to work to be an anti-racist. That is just a story, but it's how I have made sense of trauma and memory.

One thing that I have noticed through this journey, one lesson to impart, is that the *performance* of class constantly changes. Take ripped jeans. There was a time when ripped jeans were a product of a "lower" class, of an inability to replace torn clothing. Later, the style-conscious would pay high prices for the same look as a sign of privilege. In the performance of class, our parents scrimped and saved to get out of the city, and a generation later, a privileged resident must live *inside* the city—not in a suburb—to be seen as performing "high" class. My family was working class all the way—a series of plumbers, teachers, electricians, waitresses, soldiers, food vendors, and even a cop. When the plumber and the teacher took their kids from Philly to the 'burbs, they did this as a victorious act over the perils of economic competitiveness. For them, Warminster was a welcomed paradise.

Now that I am "settled down" in Cincinnati, I have a pregnant wife, young daughter and canine companions, and the whole lot of us are trying to find a house to call our own. Now that I am a family man and not a transient college kid, the view of gentrification is so much clearer. When I return for frequent visits to DC, I can see the new migrants with their fixed gear bikes, tattooed sleeves, iPhones, and giant glasses. I see them fighting for overpriced condos and dank basements converted into $1,500 a month sublets. My family is now less transient than I was in years past, and while my Ohio neighborhood now is more reflective of our family, when I return to DC to live each Spring, I am still a gentrifier. I will once again be a short-term, young renter living on the border of DC's Salvadorian, Guatemalan and Honduran *barrios*. I still do not belong. I am still an outsider making a home.

How did "Welcome to Paradise," Green Day, and punk form my identity as a nearly 30-year-old white punk? It was part of my journey, a stanza in the soundtrack to my youth. To this day I have never owned a second Green Day album, but I still count them high on the list of favorites. While I was raised on Motown, the Doors, the Beatles, and psychedelic rock, punk was the first music that I claimed for myself, my first flag planted firmly in the lunar soil that is my life. Later I became a vegan, an anarchist, and an organizer. Even farther down the line, I became a professor, husband, and father. But before it all, I was a punk.

Yes, I had a Mohawk that I would re-cut every fortnight for nearly ten years. Yes, I had (and still have) a septum ring. I consider my circle A tattoo a mark of pride, and for a time, punk tees were my uniform with a pair of Dickies and combat boots.

Punk was, and some would say still is, an oppositional identity, a rejection of something. We're not nihilists but utopians, not pro-chaos but anti-coercion. We like fast, aggressive music, a lot of us are vegan, and we all hate the State. "Making punk a threat again," the tagline of one of our newspapers, may be a bit of an oversell, but we certainly do have our roots within this proud tradition.

Did Green Day serve to gentrify punk? Did I serve to gentrify DC? How was my decision to live among largely poor and working class families while attending a private university an act of disingenuous tourism in its own right? These are the questions I have inscribed retroactively onto my days in DC and the questions raised for me by "Welcome to Paradise."

For a younger me, it was an act of political solidarity and intentional practice to challenge my sense of safety and privilege and move into an area where I was in the extreme minority. Undoubtedly, with the hindsight of the present, I can see that when white radicals move outside of their zones of racial and class comfort, our actions are not necessarily as destabilizing to "the system" as we think. To make a house your home *must* be more than appropriating poverty. It must be an intentional process where one integrates into the world around him or her and engages in the lifelong process of building community.

> Dear mother, can you hear me laughing? It's been six whole months since that I have left your home. It makes me wonder why I'm still here. For some strange reason it's now feeling like my home, and I'm never gonna go. (Armstrong, 1994)

REFERENCES

Armstrong, B. J. (1994). Welcome to paradise [Recorded by Green Day]. On *Dookie* [CD]. Burbank, CA: Reprise Records.

Schaffer, M., Schweitzer, A., Hilton, S., & Baca, A. (2012, April 27). A guide for the responsible gentrifier. *Washington City Paper.* Retrieved from http://www.washingtoncitypaper.com/articles/42565/handbook-for-the-responsible-gentrifier/

Wax, E. (2012, May 29). Gentrification spelled out: Fish in the 'hood renamed fish in the neighborhood. *Washington Post.*

ABOUT THE CONTRIBUTORS

Edward Avery-Natale received his PhD from Temple University in Philadelphia, PA in the spring of 2012 where he completed his dissertation on the topic of identification construction narratives among Philadelphia's anarcho-punk subculture. Since then he has taught at Temple University, Widener University, and La Salle University. Beginning in the fall of 2013, he will be a visiting professor at North Dakota State University in Fargo. His teaching and research interests include identification, social movements, popular and youth cultures, politics, anarchism, atheism, qualitative research methods, and critical theory.

Michael Benitez is Dean of Diversity and Inclusion and Chief Diversity Officer at the University of Puget Sound and is currently a PhD candidate in educational policy and leadership at Iowa State University. He is a highly sought out speaker and consultant with *Speak Out: The Institute for Democratic Education and Culture* and often collaborates with leading scholars and activists in social justice and diversity education. His work examines issues surrounding diversity and inclusion, systemic inequity, anti-oppressive theories and praxis, transformative pedagogy, coalition building, culture and identity politics, and knowledge production and representation.

Comrade Black is a green-anarchist community organizer who lives in Victoria B.C., the unceded traditional territories of the Lekwungen and other Coast Salish people. Comrade has organized shows for hundreds of DIY bands under the name Noise Not Bombs. They are a co-founder of the Victoria Anarchist Bookfair, a long standing member of the Camas Books

Rebel Music, pages 159–164

Collective, and have been active for many years with Food Not Bombs. Comrade corresponds with many anarchist prisoners including Walter Bond and Nyki Kish and is active in prison support, sober space organizing, animal activism, and anti-colonial organizing. Comrade is a performance poet and hosts a regular column with the longstanding anarcho-punk zine Profane Existence (profaneexistence.org).

Sarat Colling has a Master's degree in critical sociology from Brock University. Her current work examines the experience and representations of animals who have escaped from factory farms and slaughterhouses. Colling has volunteered for environmental, animal, and social justice organizations in B.C. and Ontario. She is the founder of *Political Media Review* and co-author of *Love and Liberation: An Animal Liberation Front Story.*

Lauren Corman, PhD, teaches Critical Animal Studies in the Department of Sociology at Brock University in St. Catharines, Canada. She was a host and producer of the animal advocacy radio program and podcast "Animal Voices," on CIUT 89.5 FM in Toronto 2001–2009, a show she still happily guest hosts. Her research focuses on human and nonhuman voices, subjectivities, and resistances. Her interdisciplinary scholarship and activism draws on a variety of anti-oppression theories, especially those that link animal rights and liberation struggles with other social justice and environmental concerns.

Chuck D (Carlton Ridenhour) is the leader and co-founder of the legendary Hip Hop group Public Enemy. He is also the author of two critically acclaimed books, *Fight the Power: Rap, Race, and Reality* and *Chuck D: Lyrics of a Rap Revolutionary.* Chuck D redefined rap music and Hip Hop culture with the release of Public Enemy's debut album in 1987. Most recently, his alma mater, Adelphi University, conferred Chuck D with an honorary doctorate degree and celebrated his work as a DJ at the university radio station, WBAU, a hub for the early expansion of Hip Hop music and culture.

Martha Diaz is a community organizer, media producer, curator, social entrepreneur, and adjunct professor at New York University's Gallatin School. She has been dedicated to advancing social justice and human rights, cultivating leaders and artists, and mentoring youth for 20 years. Diaz founded the Hip-Hop Odyssey International Film Festival and Hip-Hop Education Summit. She is co-editor of the *Hip-Hop Education Guidebook, Vol. I.* In 2010, Diaz founded the Hip-Hop Education Center in collaboration with New York University's Metropolitan Center—Steinhardt School. Diaz is first resident Hip-Hop Scholar at the Schomburg Center for Research in Black Culture, a NY public library.

Zack Furness is an assistant professor of communications at Penn State Greater Allegheny. He is the author of *One Less Car: Bicycling and the Politics of Automobility* (Temple University Press, 2010), editor of *Punkademics* (Minor Compositions, 2012), and co-editor of *The NFL: Critical/Cultural Perspectives* (Temple University Press, forthcoming). He has played in punk bands since 1997 and currently sings for BARONS in Pittsburgh, PA.

Ross Haenfler is an associate professor of sociology at the University of Mississippi. Growing up in the hardcore, straight edge, and punk rock scenes led to a lasting interest in youth subcultures, social justice, and DIY politics. He authored *Straight Edge: Clean Living Youth, Hardcore Punk, and Social Change* and *Goths, Gamers, and Grrrls: Deviance and Youth Subcultures.* Ross also coauthored *The Better World Handbook: Small Changes That Make a Big Difference.* An award-winning teacher, his courses include social movements, deviance, men and masculinities, and political sociology. His biggest passions, however, are his partner, Jennifer, and daughters, River and Wren.

Marcella Runell Hall is the founding co-director for the "Of Many" Institute for Multifaith Leadership and clinical instructor in the Silver School of Social Work at New York University. Hall also holds a doctorate in social justice education from the University of Massachusetts, Amherst where her research focused on Hip Hop as social justice pedagogy. Hall edited three award-winning books, *The Hip-Hop Education Guidebook, Conscious Women Rock the Page* and *Love, Race & Liberation,* and also co-founded the Hip-Hop Pedagogy Initiative at NYU. Hall resides in Bed-Stuy, Brooklyn with her husband Dave, aka DJ Trends, and their daughter, Aaliyah.

Chris Hannah is the lead singer/guitarist/songwriter for the Canadian punk band Propagandhi. Sometimes going by the name Glen Lambert to conceal his identity, or Jesus H. Chris to let everyone know just how much he bleeds for us all, Hannah's ultimate sacrifice for the greater good of the world came about back in 1986 when he co-founded the band. He was also the co-founder of the record label G7 Welcoming Committee Records and is co-host of the Escape Velocity podcast. His music, lyrics, and commentary address the full spectrum of social, political, and ethical issues in today's modern wastelands.

Daniel White Hodge, PhD, is the director of the Center for Youth Ministry Studies and an assistant professor of youth ministry at North Park University in Chicago. His research and community engagement explore the intersections of faith, critical race theory, justice, Hip Hop culture, and youth culture. His two books are *Heaven Has A Ghetto: The Missiological Gospel & Theology of Tupac Amaru Shakur* (VDM, 2009) and *The Soul Of Hip Hop: Rimbs, Timbs, & A Cultural Theology* (IVP, 2010). He is currently working on a book titled *The Hostile Gospel: Finding Religion In The Post Soul Theology of Hip Hop* (Brill, 2015).

Michael Loadenthal is a full-time dad and part-time, precariously employed, adjunct and grad student working to smash the State. Back in the day he was a Mohawked, septum-ringed, circle (A)-tattooed, anti-authoritarian teen, and is now thirty and Mohawk-less. Besides a healthy hatred of politicians and cops, Michael is a survivor of hundreds of house shows, hordes of circle pits, and the resurgence of skacore. When he's not singing his daughter to sleep to the likes of Propagandhi and NOFX, Michael likes to bike through traffic rocking to late '90s anarcho-crust and eastcoast hardcore. He also loves Hip Hop . . . but don't tell the punks.

Anthony J. Nocella II, PhD, an intersectional academic-activist, is a visiting professor in the School of Education at Hamline University and senior fellow of the Dispute Resolution Institute at the Hamline Law School. Dr. Nocella has published more than fifty scholarly articles or book chapters; co-founded eco-ability and critical animal studies; co-founded and is director of the Institute for Critical Animal Studies; is the editor of the Peace Studies Journal; and has published more than fifteen books. His areas of interest include social justice education, disability studies, Hip Hop, transformative justice, and peace and conflict studies. His website is www.anthonynocella.org.

Noelle Chaddock is a PhD candidate at Binghamton University in philosophy, interpretation and culture. Chaddock is the Director of Multicultural Life and Diversity at the State University of New York at Cortland. Chaddock also teaches at Cortland in the Africana Studies and Philosophy Departments, where she worked to have Hip Hop Philosophy become a permanent course offering and a GE. Chaddock's current research is grounded in critical race theory and specifically looks at mixed race identity and the role of intimate reality in mixed race identity development in United States Millennials.

Priya Parmar, PhD, is an associate professor of secondary education and program head of English education at Brooklyn College-CUNY. Her scholarly publications center around critical literacies, youth and Hip Hop culture, and other contemporary issues in the field of cultural studies in which economic, political, and social justice issues are addressed. Dr. Parmar is the co-founder (with Bryonn Bain) of the Lyrical Minded: Enhancing Literacy through Popular Culture & Spoken Word Poetry program working with NYC high school teachers and administrators in creating and implementing critical literacy units using popular culture, critical media literacy, and spoken-word poetry into individual classrooms across the disciplines.

Emery Petchauer, EdD, is assistant professor of teacher development and educational studies at Oakland University. His research centers on the cultural dimensions of teaching and learning, particularly in urban schools. He is the author of *Hip-Hop Culture in College Students' Lives* (Routledge, 2012) and the co-editor of *Schooling Hip-Hop: Expanding Hip-Hop Based Education Across the Curriculum* (Teachers College Press, 2013). Emery has over 15 years of experience as a DJ in Hip Hop communities.

Kirby Pringle recorded and toured as a drummer with several punk bands from 1988 through 1994, including Destroy!, Dogma Mundista, Total Chaos, Naked Aggression, and No Consent. He published a fanzine in 1987, *Shoes That Don't Fit,* and was an early contributor to *Profane Existence.* He has been a vegan since 1987 and is raising his three children as vegans. He has taught history at Los Angeles City College and California State Polytechnic University Pomona and is currently working on a project about punk rock in Mexico.

Scott Robertson is a PhD student in the Graduate School of Education and Information Sciences, University of California, Los Angeles. He currently teaches in the language arts program at Cypress Community College. He had previously taught in Spain and Japan. Prior to starting his academic and professional endeavors, Scott was the singer and bassist for two Southern California political punk bands, releasing five albums in total. Now, he brings the punk rock spirit to his research in cultural studies, critical pedagogy, and technology/media studies. He is forever indebted to his punk rock mentors from C.Hannah to C.Haun.

Dru Ryan joined the faculty at George Mason University in 1999 and in 2005 the University of the District of Columbia. His first Hip Hop course at George Mason University was named the 14th "coolest" course by *College Bound Teen* magazine. He has published across many fields and has been quoted by, among others, the *Washington Post, Washington Times, Dallas Fort Worth Star Telegram,* wired.com, *Chief Learning Officer* and *Black Engineer* magazine. Ryan is currently an executive editor for *Word, Beats, and Life: The Global Journal of Hip-Hop Culture.*

Don C. Sawyer III is currently a faculty member in the department of sociology at Quinnipiac University in Hamden, Connecticut where he is teaching the university's first sociology course dedicated to Hip Hop culture. His scholarly focus is on race, urban education, Hip Hop culture, and youth critical media literacy. His research adds to the work of scholars interested in finding solutions to the plight of students of color in failing school districts and aims to center the often silenced voices of urban youth as experts with the ability to understand and articulate their lived experiences.

Hasan Stephens, aka DJ Maestro, was born and raised in the Bronx, NY. As a DJ, he has worked at MTV, guest hosted BET Rap City and held top ratings on Clear Channel's Power 106.9 and Hot 107.9 in Syracuse, NY. Maestro was nominated for an Emmy Award for News Channel 9 (WSYR) series "Coming Together for A Safer Syracuse." Now in Syracuse, NY, he runs his company, That Good Media, has an online radio station (www.idv8radio.com), is founder of Good Life Youth Foundation (www.agoodlifefound.org) for at-risk youth and is currently the official DJ for Syracuse University for basketball and football.

David Stovall, PhD is an associate professor of educational policy studies and African-American studies at the University of Illinois at Chicago. Currently his research and community engagement investigates the intersections of critical race theory, school/community relationships, the relationship between education systems and housing markets, youth culture, community organizing, and education. In addition to his university appointment, he is also a volunteer social studies teacher at the Greater Lawndale High School for Social Justice (SOJO).

Made in the USA
Coppell, TX
26 March 2020

17673384R00107